A View of Society

France, Switzerland, and Germany

Vol. 1

With Anecdotes Relating to Some Eminent Characters

John Moore

Alpha Editions

This edition published in 2024

ISBN : 9789362926630

Design and Setting By
Alpha Editions
www.alphaedis.com
Email - info@alphaedis.com

As per information held with us this book is in Public Domain.
This book is a reproduction of an important historical work. Alpha Editions uses the best technology to reproduce historical work in the same manner it was first published to preserve its original nature. Any marks or number seen are left intentionally to preserve its true form.

Contents

LETTER I.	- 1 -
LETTER II.	- 4 -
LETTER III.	- 6 -
LETTER IV.	- 9 -
LETTER V.	- 11 -
LETTER VI.	- 13 -
LETTER VII.	- 17 -
LETTER VIII.	- 19 -
LETTER IX.	- 22 -
LETTER X.	- 24 -
LETTER XI.	- 27 -
LETTER XII.	- 31 -
LETTER XIII.	- 35 -
LETTER XIV.	- 38 -
LETTER XV.	- 42 -
LETTER XVI.	- 46 -
LETTER XVII.	- 49 -
LETTER XVIII.	- 53 -
LETTER XIX.	- 55 -
LETTER XX.	- 59 -
LETTER XXI.	- 62 -
LETTER XXII.	- 65 -
LETTER XXIII.	- 67 -
LETTER XXIV.	- 70 -
LETTER XXV.	- 75 -
LETTER XXVI.	- 80 -

LETTER XXVII.	- 83 -
LETTER XXVIII.	- 87 -
LETTER XXIX.	- 92 -
LETTER XXX.	- 97 -
LETTER XXXI.	- 101 -
LETTER XXXII.	- 106 -
LETTER XXXIII.	- 109 -
LETTER XXXIV.	- 112 -
LETTER XXXV.	- 115 -
LETTER XXXVI.	- 119 -
LETTER XXXVII.	- 122 -
LETTER XXXVIII.	- 124 -
LETTER XXXIX.	- 128 -
LETTER XL.	- 131 -
LETTER XLI.	- 134 -
LETTER XLII.	- 138 -
LETTER XLIII.	- 140 -
LETTER XLIV.	- 142 -
LETTER XLV.	- 144 -
LETTER XLVI.	- 146 -
LETTER XLVII.	- 150 -
LETTER XLVIII.	- 154 -
LETTER XLIX.	- 157 -

LETTER I.

Paris.

I was greatly disappointed by your not coming to town, as you intended, having been for some time impatient to inform you of what passed between your young friend —— and me; I relied till the moment of our departure on having an opportunity of doing this personally, and I seize the first occasion of communicating the whole to you, in the only manner now in my power.

You will remember the uneasiness you once expressed to me on account of that gentleman's propensity to gaming, and of the inconveniencies to which he had been put by some recent losses; you will also remember the resolutions which, in consequence of your request, he formed against play; but you have yet to learn, that he resumed the dice before the month was ended in which he had determined never to touch them more, and concluded one unfortunate night, by throwing away a sum far exceeding any of his former losses.

Ashamed of his weakness, he carefully concealed his misfortune from you, and thereby has been subjected to some distresses of a more mortifying nature than any he had formerly felt.

What shocked him most, was a circumstance which will not greatly astonish you—the indifference which many who call themselves his friends, showed at his situation, and the coldness with which they excused themselves from making any attempts to relieve him from his difficulties. Several to whom he had advanced considerable sums in the days of his good fortune, declared a perfect inability of repaying any part of their debt; they told some sad tale of an unforeseen accident, which had put that entirely out of their power for the present; yet one of those unfortunate gentlemen, the same evening that he refused to repay our friend, lost double the sum, every farthing of which he actually paid in ready money.

Mr. ——'s expectations from those resources having in a great measure failed, he applied to Mr. P—— in the City, who supplied him with money, at legal interest, sufficient to clear all his debts, for which he has granted him a mortgage on his estate.—While our young friend informed me of all this, he declared, that the remorse he felt on the recollection of his folly was infinitely greater than any pleasure he had ever experienced from winning, or could enjoy from the utmost success. He expressed, at the same time, a strong sense of obligation to you and to me, for our endeavours to wean him from the habit of gaming, regretted that they had not been sooner successful, but was happy to find, that he still had enough left to enable him to live in a decent manner, agreeable to a plan of œconomy which he has laid down, and to which he is resolved to adhere till the mortgage is relieved. "I have now (added he in a solemn manner) formed an ultimate resolution against gaming for the rest of my life; if I ever deviate from this, you have a right to consider me as devoid of manly firmness and truth, unworthy of your friendship, and the weakest of mortals."

Notwithstanding the young gentleman's failure on a former occasion, yet the just reflections he made on his past conduct, and the determined manner in which he spoke, give me great hopes that he will keep his present resolution.—To him I seemed fully persuaded of this, and ventured to say, that I could scarcely regret his last run of bad luck, which had operated so blessed an effect; for he who has the vigour to disentangle himself from the snares of deep play, at the expence of half his fortune, and with his character entire, may on the whole be esteemed a fortunate man. I therefore insisted strongly on the wisdom of his plan, which I contrasted with the usual determination of those who have been unlucky at play. Without fortitude to retrench their expences, or bear their first misfortunes, they can only bring themselves the length of resolving to renounce gaming *as soon as they shall regain what they have lost*; and imagining they have still a claim to the money which is now in the pockets of others, because it was once in their own, they throw away their whole fortune in search of an inconsiderable part, and finish by being completely ruined, because they could not support a small inconvenience. I pointed out, how infinitely more honourable it was to depend for repairing his fortune on his own good sense and perseverance, than on the revolutions of chance; which, even if they should be favourable, could only re-establish him at the expence of others, most probably of those who had no hand in occasioning his losses. His inseparable companion —— —— entered while I was in the middle of my harangue. Our friend, who had previously acquainted him with his determination of renouncing gaming, endeavoured to prevail on that gentleman to adopt the same measure, but in vain. —— —— laughed at his proposal, said, "he was too easily terrified; that one tolerable run of good fortune would retrieve his affairs; that my fears about ruin were mere bugbears; that the word *ruin*, like cannon charged with powder, had an alarming sound, but was attended with no danger; that if the worst should happen, I could but be ruined; which was only being in the same situation with some of the most fashionable people in the nation."

He then enumerated many instances of those who lived as well as the wealthiest men in England, and yet every body pronounced them ruined. "There is Ch—— F——, added he, a man completely ruined; yet beloved by his friends, and admired by his country as much as ever."

To this fine reasoning I replied, "That if nobody had been influenced by that gentleman's example, except those who possessed his genius, his turn for play would never have hurt one man in the kingdom; but that those who owed their importance solely to their fortune, ought not to risk it so wantonly as he might do, whose fortune had always been of little importance, when compared with his abilities; and since they could not imitate Mr. F—— in the things for which he was so justly applauded, they ought not to follow his example in those for which he was as justly condemned; for the same fire which burns a piece of wood to ashes, can only melt a guinea, which still retains its intrinsic value, *though his Majesty's countenance no longer shines upon it.*"

—— —— did not seem to relish my argument, and soon after left us; but our young friend seemed confirmed in his resolutions, and gave me fresh assurances, the day on which I left London, that he never would vary.

Knowing the interest you take in his welfare, and the high esteem he has for you, I have thought it right to give you this piece of information which I know will afford you pleasure. His greatest difficulty in adhering to the new adopted plan will be at first; in his present state of mind, the soothings and support of friendship may be of the greatest service.

When your affairs permit you to go to London, I dare say you will take the earliest opportunity of throwing yourself in his way: You will find no difficulty in persuading him to accompany you to the country. Removed for some months from his present companions and usual lounging-places, the influence of his old habits will gradually diminish; and, confirmed by your conversation, small chance will remain of his being sucked into the old system, and again whirled round in the vortex of dissipation and gaming.

LETTER II.

Paris.

Your setting out for London immediately on the receipt of my letter, is what might have been expected.—Nothing renders a man so active as an eager desire of doing good; and I might have foreseen, that you would catch at the opportunity with which I furnished you to indulge a ruling passion.

It gives me great satisfaction to know, that our young friend and you are upon such a confidential footing; and I heartily hope that nothing will interrupt a connection which must be a source of pleasing reflection to you, and in every way advantageous to him.—I had no doubt that he would readily agree to accompany you to the country; but I was not so certain that he might not have found it necessary to accept of your other very friendly proposal.—His refusal is a proof, that he has reconciled his mind to his circumstances; and, with those sentiments, I am convinced that he will be able to live within his remaining yearly income with more satisfaction than he enjoyed when he spent five times that sum.—

You insist so much on my writing to you regularly, from the different places where I may reside during my absence from England, that I begin to believe you are in earnest, and shall certainly obey your commands.

I know you do not expect from me a minute account of churches and palaces. However agreeable these may be to the spectator, they generally afford but a slender entertainment when served up in description.

There are countries, some of which I may again visit before my return to England, whose appearance always strikes the eye with delight; but it is difficult to convey a precise idea of their beauties in words. The pencil is a more powerful vehicle than the pen for that purpose; for the landscape is apt to vanish from the mind before the description can be read.

The manners, customs, and characters of the people may probably furnish the chief materials in the correspondence you exact, with such reflections as may arise from the subject. In these, I apprise you before-hand, I shall take what latitude I please: And though the complexion of my letters may most probably receive some tint or shade of colouring from the country where they may be wrote; yet if I take it into my head to insist on the little tricks of an attorney, when you expect to hear of the politics of a prime minister; or, if I tell you a tale about an old woman, when you are impatient for anecdotes of a great general, you must not fret or fall into a passion; for if you do not permit me to write on what subjects I please, and treat them in my own way, the correspondence you require would become a sad slavery to me, and of consequence no amusement to you. Whereas, if you leave me free and unrestrained, it will at least form some occupation to myself, may wean me from the habit of lounging, and will afford an excuse, in my own mind, for my leaving those parties of pleasure where people are apt to continue, forcing smiles, and yawning spontaneously for two or three hours after all relish is fled.

Yet in this dismal condition many remain night after night, because the hour of sleep is not yet arrived;—and what else can they do?

Have you never found yourself in this listless situation? Without any pleasure where you are, without any motive to be gone, you remain in a kind of passive, gaping oyster-state, till the tide of the company moves you to your carriage. And when you recover your reflection in your bed-chamber, you find you have passed the two last hours in a kind of humming buzzing stupor, without satisfaction, or ideas of any kind.

I thank you for your offer of Dupont. Knowing your regard for him, and his dexterity and intelligence in the science of valet-de-chambreship, I see the full force of the sacrifice you are willing to make. If I could be so selfish on another occasion as to accept your offer, the good-will I bear to your old friend John would prevent me at present. Dupont, to be sure, is worth twenty of John for that employment; but I can never forget his long attachment, and I am now so habituated to him, that one generally esteemed a more perfect servant would not suit me so well. I think myself benefited even by his deficiencies, which have obliged me to do many things for myself that other people perform by the hands of their servants. Many of our acquaintances seem absolutely incapable of motion, till they have been wound up by their valets. They have no more use of their hands for any office about their own persons, than if they were paralytic. At night they must wait for their servants, before they can undress themselves, and go to bed: In the morning, if the valet happen to be out of the way, the master must remain helpless and sprawling in bed, like a turtle on its back upon the kitchen-table of an alderman.

I remain, &c.

LETTER III.

Paris.

I Went a few nights since to the Italian Comedy; while I enjoyed the exquisite *naiveté* of my old friend Carlin, the Marquis de F——, whom you have seen at London, entered the box:—He flew to me with all the vivacity of a Frenchman, and with every mark of pleasure and regard. He had ten thousand questions to ask about his friends in England all in one breath, and without waiting for an answer. Mon cher ami this, ma chere amie t'other; la belle such a one, la charmante such another.

Perceiving we disturbed the company, and having no hopes that the Marquis would be more quiet for some time, I proposed leaving the Comedy. He assented immediately:—Vous avez raison: il n'y a personne ici; c'est un désert—(by the way, the house was very much crowded)—Je suis venu comme vous voyez en polisson;—tout le monde est au Colisée—Allons.— We stepped into his vis-à-vis: He ordered the coachman to drive vîte comme tous les diables. The horses went as fast as they could, and the Marquis's tongue still faster than they.

When we arrived, I proposed going up to the gallery, where we might see the company below, and converse without interruption, Bon, says he, nous nous nicherons dans un coin pour critiquer tout le monde, comme deux diables boiteux.

A lady of a fine shape and majestic air drew my attention: I asked the Marquis if he did not think her remarkably handsome?—Là, là, said he, coldly.—Nous sommes heureusement placés pour elle. C'est un tableau fait pour être vu de loin.—I then took notice of the excessive whiteness of her skin.—C'est apparemment le goût de son amant d'aujourd'hui, said he; et quand un autre se présenteroit qui préféreroit la couleur de puce, à l'aide d'un peu d'eau chaude, elle seroit aussi son affaire.

I next remarked two ladies dressed a little beyond the extravagance of the mode. Their features betrayed the approach of fifty, in spite of all the art which had evidently been used to conceal that hated age.

At sight of them the Marquis started up. Ah! parblieu, said he, ces deux morceaux d'antiquité sont de mes parentes.—Excusez moi pour deux minutes: il faut que je m'approche d'elles, pour les féliciter de leurs appas. Old ladies, continued he, who have the rage to be thought young, are of all animals the most vindictive when neglected, and I have particular reasons for wishing to remain in their good graces. He then left me, and having walked round the circle with the ladies, returned and took his seat. I have got myself well out of the scrape, said he; I told them I was engaged with a Milord, whom I should have the honour of presenting at their house; and I fixed a young officer with them, whose best hopes of promotion depend upon their influence at court, and who dares as soon quit his colours in battle, as forsake these two pieces of old tapestry till they chuse to retire.

A young man very magnificently dressed entered the room: He announced his importance by his airs, his bustle, the loud and decisive tone of his voice. The Marquis told me, it was Mons. le Duc de ———; that it was indispensably necessary that I should be presented to him; there was no living at Paris without that advantage; adding,—Il est un peu fat, infiniment bête; d'ailleurs le meilleur enfant du monde.

A fine lady next appeared who seemed to command the admiration of the whole assembly. She floated round the circle of the Colisée, surrounded by a cluster of Petits Maitres, whose eyes were fixed on her, and who seemed moved by her motion, like satellites under the influence of their planet. She, on her part, was perfectly serene, and unembarrassed by the attention and the eyes of the spectators. She smiled to one, nodded to another, shrugged to a third, struck a fourth with her fan, burst into a fit of laughter to a fifth, and whispered in the ear of a sixth. All these, and a thousand tricks more, she ran through with the ease of an actress and the rapidity of a juggler. She seemed fully persuaded that she was the only person present worthy of attention; that it belonged to her to develop her charms, display her graces and airs, and that it was the part of the rest of the company to remain attentive and admiring spectators.

Cette drolesse là, said the Marquis, est jolie, et pour cette raison on croit qu'elle a de l'esprit: On a même tâché de répéter ses bons mots; mais ils ne sont faits que pour sa bouche. Elle est beaucoup plus vaine que sensible, grand soutien pour sa vertu! au reste, elle est dame de qualité, à la faveur de quoi elle possede un goût de hardiesse si heureux, qu'elle jouit du bénéfice de l'effronterie sans être effrontée.

I was surprised to find all this satire directed against so beautiful a woman, and suspected that the edge of F———'s remarks was sharpened by some recent pique. I was going to rally him on that supposition, when he suddenly started up, saying, Voilà Mons. de ———, le meilleur de mes amis.—Il est aimable; on ne peut pas plus.—Il a de l'esprit comme un démon.—Il faut que vous le connoissiez. Allons:—Descendons. So saying, he hurried me down stairs, presented me to Mons. de ——— as un philosophe Anglois, who understood race-horses better than the great Newton himself, and who had no aversion to the game of Whist. Mons. de ——— received me with open arms, and we were intimate friends in ten minutes. He carried the Marquis and me to sup at his house, where he found a numerous company.

The conversation was cheerful and animated. There were some very ingenious men present, with an admirable mixture of agreeable women, who remained to the last, and joined in the conversation even when it turned on subjects of literature; upon which occasions English ladies generally imagine it becomes them to remain silent. But here they took their share without scruple or hesitation. Those who understood any thing of the subject delivered their sentiments with great precision, and more grace than the men; those who knew nothing of the matter rallied their own ignorance in such a sprightly manner, as convinced every body, that knowledge is not necessary to render a woman exceedingly agreeable in society.

After passing a most delightful evening, I returned to my lodgings, my head undisturbed with wine, and my spirits unjaded by play.

LETTER IV.

Paris.

We have been a month at Paris; a longer time than was intended at our arrival: yet our departure appears to me at a greater distance now than it did then.

F—— has been my most constant companion; he is universally liked, lives in the very best company, and whoever is introduced by him is sure of a favourable reception. I found little or no difficulty in excusing myself from play. The Marquis undertook to make this matter easy; and nothing can be a greater proof of his influence in some of the most fashionable circles, than his being able to introduce a man without a title, and who never games.

He is also intimately acquainted with some of the most eminent men of letters, to whom he has made me known. Many of those, whose works you admire, are received at the houses of the first nobility on the most liberal footing.

You can scarcely believe the influence which this body of men have in the gay and dissipated city of Paris. Their opinions not only determine the merit of works of taste and science, but they have considerable weight on the manners and sentiments of people of rank, of the public in general, and consequently are not without effect on the measures of government.

The same thing takes place in some degree in most countries of Europe; but, if I am not mistaken, more at Paris than any where else; because men of letters are here at once united to each other by the various academies, and diffused among private societies, by the manners and general taste of the nation.

As the sentiments and conversation of men of letters influence, to a certain degree, the opinions and the conduct of the fashionable world; the manners of these last have a more obvious effect upon the air, the behaviour, and the conversation of the former, which in general is polite and easy; equally purified from the awkward timidity contracted in retirement, and the disgusting arrogance inspired by university honours, or church dignities. At Paris, the pedants of Moliere are to be seen on the stage only.

In this country, at present, there are many men distinguished by their learning, who at the same time are cheerful and easy in mixed company, unpresuming in argument, and in every respect as well bred as those who have no other pretension.

Politeness and good manners, indeed, may be traced, though in different proportions, through every rank, from the greatest of the nobility to the lowest mechanic. This forms a more remarkable and distinguishing feature in the French national character, than the vivacity, impetuosity, and fickleness, for which the ancient as well as the modern inhabitants of this country have been noted.—It certainly is a very singular phænomenon, that politeness, which in every other country is confined to people of a certain rank in life, should here pervade every situation and profession. The man in power is courteous to his dependant, the prosperous to the unfortunate, the very beggar who solicits charity, does it 'en homme comme il faut;' and if his request be not granted, he is sure, at least, that it will be refused with an appearance of humanity, and not with harshness or insult.

A stranger, quite new and unversed in their language, whose accent is uncouth and ridiculous in the ears of the French, and who can scarcely open his mouth without making a blunder in grammar or idiom, is heard with the most serious attention, and never laughed at, even when he utters the oddest solecism or equivocal expression.

I am afraid, said I, yesterday, to a French gentleman, the phrase which I used just now is not French. Monsieur, replied he, cette expression effectivement n'est pas Françoise, mais elle mérite bien de l'être.

The most daring deviation from fashion, in the important article of dress, cannot make them forget the laws of good-breeding. When a person appears at the public walks, in clothes made against every law of the mode, upon which the French are supposed to lay such stress, they do not gaze or sneer at him; they allow him first to pass, as it were, unobserved, and do not till then turn round to indulge the curiosity which his uncommon figure may have excited. I have remarked this instance of delicacy often in the streets in the lowest of the vulgar, or rather of the common people; for there are really very few of the natives of Paris, who can be called vulgar.

There are exceptions to these, as to all general remarks on the manners and character of any nation.

I have heard instances of the military treating postillions and inn-keepers with injustice; and the seigneur or intendant oppressing the peasant. Examples of the abuse of power, and insolence of office, are to be met with every where. If they are tolerated, the fault lies in the government.

I have not been speaking of the French government. Their national character is one thing; the nature of their government is a very different matter. But I am convinced there is no country in Europe where royal favour, high birth, and the military profession, could be allowed such privileges as they have in France, and where there would be so few instances of their producing rough and brutal behaviour to inferiors.

LETTER V.

Paris.

A candid Englishman, of whatever rank in life he may be, must see with indignation, that every thing in this kingdom is arranged for the accommodation of the rich and the powerful; and that little or no regard is paid to the comfort of citizens of an inferior station. This appears in a thousand instances, and strikes the eye immediately on entering Paris.

I think I have seen it somewhere remarked, that the regular and effectual manner in which the city of London is lighted at night, and the raised pavements on the sides of every street, for the security and conveniency of foot passengers, seem to indicate, that the body of the people, as well as the rich and great, are counted of some importance in the eye of government. Whereas Paris is poorly and partially lighted; and except on the Pont Neuf and Pont Royal, and the keys between them, is not provided with foot-ways for the accommodation and safety of those who cannot afford carriages. They must therefore grope their way as they best can, and skulk behind pillars, or run into shops, to avoid being crushed by the coaches, which are driven as near the wall as the coachman pleases; dispersing the people on foot at their approach, like chaff before the wind.

It must be acknowledged, that monarchy (for the French do not love to hear it called despotism, and it is needless to quarrel with them about a word) is raised in this country so very high, that it quite loses sight of the bulk of the nation, and pays attention only to a few; who, being in exalted stations, come within the Court's sphere of vision.

Le peuple, in France, is a term of reproach.—Un homme du peuple, implies a want of both education and manners. Un homme comme il faut, on the other hand, does not imply a man of sense or principle, but simply a man of birth or fashion; for a man may be homme comme il faut, and yet be devoid of every quality which adorns human nature. There is no question that government leaves the middle and inferior ranks of life in some degree unprotected, and exposed to the injustice and insolence of the great; who are considered in this country, as somewhat above the Law, though greatly below the Monarch.

But the polished mildness of French manners, the gay and sociable turn of the nation, the affable and easy conduct of masters to their servants, supply the deficiencies, and correct the errors, of the government, and render the condition of the common people in France, but particularly at Paris, better than in several other countries of Europe; and much more tolerable than it would be, if the national character resembled that of those countries.

I was interrupted by Lord M. who arrived last night. He agreed to dine with us. F—— called soon after: he was disengaged also, and promised to be of the party.

You know how laborious a thing it is to keep alive a dialogue with my Lord M. The conversation either degenerates into a soliloquy on your part, or expires altogether. I was therefore exceedingly happy with the thoughts of the Marquis's company. He was uncommonly lively; addressed much of his conversation to his Lordship; tried him upon every subject, wine, women, horses, politics, and religion. He then sung Chansons à boire, and endeavoured in vain to get my Lord to join in the chorus. Nothing would do.—He admired his clothes, praised his dog, and said a thousand obliging things of the English nation. To no purpose; his Lordship kept up his silence and reserve to the last, and then drove away to the opera.

Ma foi, said the Marquis, as soon as he went out of the room, il a de grands talens pour le silence, ce Milord là.

LETTER VI.

Paris.

In a former letter, I mentioned good breeding as a striking part of the French national character. Loyalty, or an uncommon fondness for, and attachment to, the persons of their princes, is another.

An Englishman, though he views the virtues of his king with a jealous eye during his reign, yet he will do them all justice in the reign of his successor.

A German, while he is silent with respect to the foibles of his prince, admires all his talents much more than he would the same qualities in any other person.

A Turk, or Persian, contemplates his Emperor with fear and reverence, as a superior being, to whose pleasure it is his duty to submit, as to the laws of Nature, and the will of Providence.

But a Frenchman, while he knows that his king is of the same nature, and liable to all the weaknesses of other men; while he enumerates his follies, and laughs as he laments them, is nevertheless attached to him by a sentiment of equal respect and tenderness; a kind of affectionate prejudice, independent of his real character.

Roi[1] is a word which conveys to the minds of Frenchmen the ideas of benevolence, gratitude, and love; as well as those of power, grandeur, and happiness.

They flock to Versailles every Sunday, behold him with unsated curiosity, and gaze on him with as much satisfaction the twentieth time as the first.

They consider him as their friend, though he does not know their persons; as their protector, though their greatest danger is from an Exempt or Lettre de Cachet; and as their benefactor, while they are oppressed with taxes.

They magnify into importance his most indifferent actions; they palliate and excuse all his weaknesses; and they impute his errors or crimes, to his ministers or other evil counsellors; who (as they fondly assert) have, for some base purpose, imposed upon his judgment, and perverted the undeviating rectitude of his intentions.

They repeat, with fond applause, every saying of his which seems to indicate the smallest approach to wit, or even bears the mark of ordinary sagacity.

The most inconsiderable circumstance which relates to the Monarch is of importance: whether he eat much or little at dinner; the coat he wears, the horse on which he rides, all afford matter of conversation in the various societies at Paris, and are the most agreeable subjects of epistolary correspondence with their friends in the provinces.

If he happens to be a little indisposed, all Paris, all France, is alarmed, as if a real calamity was threatened: and to seem interested, or to converse upon any other subject till this has been discussed, would be considered as a proof of unpardonable indifference.

At a review, the troops perform their manœuvres unheeded by such of the spectators as are within sight of the King. They are all engrossed in contemplation of their Prince.—Avez vous vu le roi?—Tenez—ah!—voilà le roi.—Le roi rit.—Apparemment il est content.—Je suis charmé,—ah, il tousse!—A-t-il toussé?—Oui, parbleu! et bien fort.—Je suis au désespoir.

At mass, it is the King, not the Priest, who is the object of attention. The Host is elevated; but the people's eyes remain fixed upon the face of their beloved Monarch.

Even the most applauded pieces of the theatre, which in Paris create more emotion than the ceremonies of religion, can with difficulty divide their attention. A smile from the King makes them forget the sorrow of Andromaché, and the wrongs of the Cid.

This excessive attachment is not confined to the person of the Monarch, but extends to every branch of the royal family; all of whom, it is imagined in this country, have an hereditary right to every gratification and enjoyment that human nature is capable of receiving. And if any cause, moral or physical, impede or obstruct this, they meet with universal sympathy. The most trivial disappointment or chagrin which befals them, is considered as more serious and affecting, than the most dreadful calamity, which can happen to a private family. It is lamented as if the natural order of things were counteracted, and the amiable Prince, or Princess, deprived, by a cruel phænomenon, of that supreme degree of happiness, to which their rank in life gives them an undeniable title.

All this regard seems real, and not affected from any motive of interest; at least it must be so with respect to the bulk of the people, who can have no hopes of ever being known to their princes, far less of ever receiving any personal favour from them.

The philosophical idea, that Kings have been appointed for public conveniency; that they are accountable to their subjects for mal-administration, or for continued acts of injustice and oppression; is a doctrine very opposite to the general prejudices of this nation. If any of their kings were to behave in such an imprudent and outrageous manner as to occasion a revolt, and if the insurgents actually got the better, I question if they would think of new-modelling the government, and limiting the power of the crown, as was done in Britain at the Revolution, so as to prevent the like abuses for the future. They never would think of going further, I imagine, than placing another prince of the Bourbon family on the throne, with the same power that his predecessor had, and then quietly lay down their arms, satisfied with his royal word or declaration to govern with more equity.

The French seem so delighted and dazzled with the lustre of Monarchy, that they cannot bear the thoughts of any qualifying mixture, which might abate its violence, and render its ardour more benign. They chuse to give the splendid machine full play, though it often scorches and threatens to consume themselves and their effects.

They consider the power of the king, from which their servitude proceeds, as if it were their own power. You will hardly believe it; but I am sure of the fact: They are proud of it; they are proud that there is no check or limitation to his authority.

They tell you with exultation, that the king has an army of near two hundred thousand men in the time of peace. A Frenchman is as vain of the palaces, fine gardens, number of horses, and all the paraphernalia belonging to the court of the Monarch, as an Englishman can be of his own house, gardens, and equipage.

When they are told of the diffusion of wealth in England, the immense fortunes made by many individuals, the affluence of those of middle rank, the security and easy situation of the common people; instead of being mortified by the comparison which might naturally occur to their imaginations, they comfort themselves with the reflection, that the court of France is more brilliant than the court of Great Britain, and that the duke of Orleans and the Prince of Condé have greater revenues than any of the English nobility.

When they hear of the freedom of debate in parliament, of the liberties taken in writing or speaking of the conduct of the king, or measures of government, and the forms to be observed, before those who venture on the most daring abuse of either can be brought to punishment, they seem filled with indignation, and say with an air of triumph, C'est bien autrement chez nous: Si le Roi de France avoit affaire à ces Messieurs là, il leur apprendroit à vivre. And then they would proceed to inform you, that, parbleu! their minister would give himself no trouble about forms or proofs; that suspicion was sufficient for him, and without more ado he would shut up such impertinent people in the Bastille for many years. And then raising their voices, as if what they said were a proof of the courage or magnanimity of the minister—Ou peut-être il feroit condamner ces drôles là aux galères pour la vie.

[1] We translate le Roi, by 'the King,' which is by no means equivalent. Le Roi does himself, and makes others do, what he pleases. The King cannot do what he pleases, but does what others please.

LETTER VII.

Paris.

It would be almost superfluous to observe, that there are a great many people in France, who think in a very different manner from that which I have mentioned in my last, and who have just and liberal ideas of the design and nature of government, and proper and manly sentiments of the natural rights of mankind. The writings of Montesquieu are greatly admired: This alone is sufficient to prove it. Many later authors, and the conversation of the philosophical and reasoning people, display the same spirit.

What is mentioned in my last letter, however, comprehends the general turn or manner of thinking of the French nation, and evinces how very opposite their sentiments upon the subject of civil government are, to those of our countrymen.

I have heard an Englishman enumerate the advantages of the British constitution to a circle of French Bourgeois, and explain to them in what manner the people of their rank of life were protected from the insolence of the courtiers and nobility; that the poorest shop-keeper and lowest tradesman in England, could have immediate redress for any injury done him by the greatest nobleman in the kingdom.

Well, what impression do you think this declamation had upon the French auditory? You will naturally imagine they would admire such a constitution, and wish for the same in France:—Not at all. They sympathized with the great: They seemed to feel for their want of importance. One observed, C'est peu de chose d'être noble chez vous; and another, shaking his head, added, Ce n'est pas naturel tout cela.

When mention was made that the king of Great Britain could not impose a tax by his own authority; that the consent of parliament, particularly of the house of commons, was necessary, to which assembly people of their rank of life were admitted; they said with some degree of satisfaction, Cependant, c'est assez beau cela. But when the English patriot, expecting their complete approbation, continued informing them, that the king himself had not the power to encroach upon the liberty of the meanest of his subjects; that if he or the minister did, damages were recoverable at a court of law, a loud and prolonged DIABLE issued from every mouth. They forgot their own situation, and the security of the people, and turned to their natural bias of sympathy with the King, who they all seemed to think must be the most oppressed and injured of mankind.

One of them at last, addressing himself to the English politician, said, Tout ce que je puis vous dire, Monsieur, c'est que votre pauvre Roi est bien à plaindre.

This solicitude of theirs for the happiness and glory of royalty extends in some degree to all crowned heads whatever: But with regard to their own monarch, it seems the reigning and darling passion of their souls, which they carry with them to the grave.

A French soldier, who lay covered with wounds on the field of Dettingen, demanded, a little before he expired, of an English officer, how the battle was likely to terminate; and being answered, that the British troops had obtained a great victory; Mon pauvre Roi, said the dying man, que fera-t-il?

For my part, my friend, although I heartily wish his Majesty all public and domestic happiness, yet if the smallest solicitude about either should disturb my dying moments, it will be the strongest proof that my own affairs, spiritual and temporal, your concerns, as well as those of my other private friends, are in a most comfortable situation.

Adieu.

P. S. I have not seen the Marquis for several days. He had informed me, at our very first meeting, that he was paying his court to a young lady of family, at his mother's desire, who was impatient to see him married. He said, he could refuse his mother nothing, parcequ'elle étoit le meilleur enfant du monde: Besides, he said, the young lady was very pretty and agreeable, and he was over head and ears in love with her. He has told me since, that every thing was arranged, and he expected to be in a short time the happiest man in the world, and would have the honour of presenting me to his bride very soon. I shall let you know my opinion of the lady when I see her—But let her be what she will, I am sorry that F—— thinks of marrying so early in life; for a Frenchman of five and twenty, is not quite so sedate an animal as an Englishman of fifteen.

LETTER VIII.

Paris.

There is an absolute penury of public news. I have nothing particular to inform you of concerning myself; but you hold me to my engagement: So here I am seated to write to you, without having as yet determined upon a subject, in hopes, however, that my pen may gather materials as it moves.

In whatever light this prejudice in favour of monarchy may appear to the eye of philosophy; and though of all passions the love of a King, merely because he is a King, is perhaps the silliest; yet it surely ought to be considered as meritorious by those who are the objects of it.

No people existing, or who did ever exist, have had so just a claim to the gratitude and affections of their sovereign, as the French. They rejoice in his joy, are grieved at his grief, proud of his power, vain of his accomplishments, indulgent to his failings. They cheerfully yield their own conveniences to his superfluities, and are at all times willing to sacrifice their lives for his glory.

A King, one would imagine, must be a perfect monster of selfishness and insensibility, who did not love such subjects, and who did not bestow some time and attention to promote their happiness: Yet the French nation has not had a Monarch worthy of all this regard since the days of Henry IV. and of all their kings they used him the worst.

Of the three brothers who immediately preceded him, the first was a sickly creature, as feeble in mind as in body; the second, a monster of superstition and cruelty; and the third, after a dawn of some brightness, allowed his meridian to be obscured by the grossest clouds of effeminacy and voluptuousness. Their Italian mother, who governed all the three, seems to have been perfectly unrestrained by any feelings of humanity or of conscience, and solely guided by motives of interest, and the most perfidious policy.

The princes who have succeeded, as well as those who reigned before the fourth Henry, serve as foils which display his bright qualities with double lustre.

Notwithstanding all the inducements which the French Kings have to promote the happiness of their subjects, it may be many centuries before they are blessed with one who shall have that passion in such a high degree.

A character in which the great and amiable virtues are so finely blended, is very rarely produced in any nation. How small then must be the chance that this prize shall fall to the individual who is destined for the throne? Henry received an education very different from that which is generally bestowed on Kings. His character was formed in the hardy school of adversity: his mind was strengthened by continual exertions of courage and prudence. He was taught humanity by suffering under the rod of tyranny, and experiencing the pangs of the unfortunate. Having frequently stood in need of friends, he knew the value of their attachment, and his heart became capable of friendship.

Difficulties and dangers often strike out particles of genius which otherwise might remain latent and useless, and contribute to the formation of a vigorous character, by animating those sparks of virtue which a life of indolence would have completely extinguished.

Those people who, from their earliest infancy, have found every thing provided for them, who have not much ambition, and consequently are seldom excited to any great exertion of their faculties, generally feel these faculties dwindle and grow weak, for the same reason that a man's arms would become gradually feeble, and at length perfectly useless, if he were to wear them in a scarf for any considerable time.

That the faculties of the understanding, like the sinews of the body, are relaxed by sloth and strengthened by exercise, nobody will doubt. I imagine the same analogy holds in some degree between the body and the qualities of the heart. Benevolence, pity, gratitude, are, I suspect, exceedingly apt to stagnate into a calm, sluggish insensibility in that breast which has not been agitated by real misfortunes.

People do not fully enter into distresses which they never have felt, and which they think they run but a small risk of feeling. Accordingly it has been remarked, that those who have been favoured through life with the smiles of fortune, and whose time has been spent in the amusements of courts, and luxurious indulgences, very often acquire an astonishing insensibility to the misfortunes of others. The character the most perfectly cold of all I ever knew, devoid of friendship, gratitude, and even natural affection, belongs to a person, whose life has been a continued series of fortunate events.

Yet while all their cares are contracted, and all their feelings absorbed, within the compass of their own skin, such people seem often convinced, that they themselves are of the most humane dispositions, and the most extensive benevolence, upon no better foundation, than because they have felt themselves affected by the artful distresses of a romance, and because they could shed a few barren tears at a tragedy.

If to these symptoms of sensibility, they can add, that of having occasionally given a guinea when the contribution has been set a going, or have parted with a little superfluous money to free themselves from importunity, they have then carried benevolence to the utmost length of *their* idea of that virtue.

They have no notion of any thing beyond this; nor would they make one active exertion, postpone a single party of pleasure, or in any shape interrupt the tranquillity of their own indolence, to perform the most essential service (I will not say to a friend, such people can have none) to any of the human race.

There are many exceptions, but in general those persons who are exposed to *the slings and arrows of outrageous fortune*, who have experienced the base indifference of mankind, and have in some degree *felt what wretches feel*, are endued with the truest sympathy, and enter, with the most lively sensibility, into the situation of the unfortunate.

   Non ignara mali, miseris succurrere disco,

said Dido, who had been obliged to fly from her country, to Æneas, who had been witness to the destruction of his.

Dido and Æneas!—How in the name of wandering have we got into their company? I could no more have guessed at this, than at the subject of one of Montaigne's Essays from the title. We set out, I believe, with something about France;—but you cannot expect that I should attempt to take up a thread which is left so far behind.

Adieu.

LETTER IX.

Paris.

I mentioned in a former letter, that my friend F—— was on the point of being married. He called at my lodgings a little while ago. His air was so very gay, that I imagined he had some agreeable news to communicate. Me voilà au désespoir, mon cher ami, said he, with a loud laugh.—You are the merriest man I ever saw in that situation, said I.—He then informed me, that the old Marquis de P. his mistress's father, had waited on his mother, and, after ten thousand apologies and circumlocutions, had given her to understand, that certain things had intervened, which rendered it impossible that he should ever have the honour of being father-in-law to her son; and requested her to inform him, how infinitely uneasy he and all his family were, at an incident which deprived them of the pleasure they had proposed to themselves from that connection. His mother, he said, had endeavoured to discover the incident which has produced this sudden alteration;—but to no purpose.— The old gentleman contented himself with assuring her, that the particulars would be equally disagreeable and superfluous,—and then took his leave, in the most polite and affectionate terms that the French language could furnish him with.

F—— told me all this with an air so easy and contented, that I did not well know what to make of it. My dear Marquis, said I, it is fortunate that I have been mistaken; for you must know, I had taken it into my head that you were fond of the lady.—You were in the right, my friend, said he, je l'aimois infiniment.—Comment infiniment; said I, and yet be so merry when you are just going to lose her!—Mais vous autres Anglois, said he, vous avez des idées si bizarres!—aimer infiniment, cela veut dire aimer comme on aime,— tout le monde s'aime ainsi quand il ne se hait pas,—Mais je vous conterai toute l'histoire.

My mother, added he, who is the best creature in the world, and whom I love with all my soul, told me this marriage would make her quite happy.—All my uncles and aunts, and cousins, for ten generations, told me the same. I was informed, over and above, that the lady, her father, and all their relations, wished this alliance, with the most obliging earnestness. The girl, herself, is tolerably pretty. They will persuade me to marry some time or other, thought I; why not now, as well as at another time? Why should I refuse to do a thing which will please so many people, without being in the smallest degree displeasing to myself?—To be sure, said I, that would have been ill-natured. It was lucky, however, that you happened to be perfectly disengaged, and did not prefer any other woman.

You are mistaken, my friend, said he; I preferred many to the lady in question, and one in particular, whose name I will not mention, but whom I love—whom I do love.—Comme on aime, said I, interrupting him.—Non, parbleu! added he, with warmth, comme on n'aime pas.—Good Heaven! then, cried I, how could you think of marrying another?—Celà n'empêche rien, said the Marquis, coolly;—for I could not marry the other. She had the start of me, and had undergone the ceremony already; and therefore she had no objection to my obliging my mother and relations in this particular, for she is the best-natured woman in the world.

So she appears to be, said I.—O, pour cela oui, mon cher, added he, elle est la bonté même. However, I am very well pleased, upon the whole, that the affair has gone off without any fault of mine; and though it is possible that it may be brought on at some future period, I shall still be a gainer, parceque un mariage reculé est toujours autant de gagné sur le repentir. So saying, he wheeled on his heel, humming,

Non, tu ne le mettra pas, Colin, &c.

There's the picture of a French lover for you.—I set down the whole scene, as soon as F—— left me, and so I leave you to make your own reflections.

Adieu.

LETTER X.

Paris.

You have often heard the French accused of insincerity, and of being warm in professions, but devoid of real friendship.

Our countrymen, in particular, are led into this opinion, from the manners in general being more obsequious here, than in England. What Frenchmen consider as common good manners, many Englishmen would call flattery, perhaps fawning.

Their language abounds in complimental phrases, which they distribute with wonderful profusion and volubility; but they intend no more by them, than an Englishman means when he subscribes himself your most obedient humble servant, at the conclusion of a letter.

A Frenchman not only means nothing beyond common civility, by the plentiful shower of compliments which he pours on every stranger; but also, he takes it for granted, that the stranger knows that nothing more is meant. These expressions are fully understood by his own countrymen: he imagines all the world are as well informed; and he has not the smallest intention to deceive. But if any man takes these expressions in a literal sense, and believes that people are in reality inspired with friendship, or have fallen in love with him at first sight, he will be very much disappointed; especially if he expects strong proofs of either.

Yet he has no right to accuse the French of insincerity, or breach of friendship.—Friendship is intirely out of the question. They never intended to convey any other idea, than that they were willing to receive him on the footing of an acquaintance;—and it was the business of his language-master to have informed him of the real import of their expressions.

If the same words indeed were literally translated into English, and used by one Englishman to another, the person to whom they were addressed, would have good reason to imagine that the other had a particular regard for him, or meant to deceive him; because the established modes of civility and politeness in England do not require such language.

The not making a proper allowance for different modes and usages which accident has established, is one great cause of the unfavourable and harsh sentiments, which the people of the different countries of the world too often harbour against each other.

You may say, perhaps, that this superfluity of compliments which the French make use of, is a proof of the matter in question; that the French have less sincerity than their neighbours. By the same rule we must conclude, that the common people of every nation, who use few complimental phrases in their discourse, have a greater regard to truth, and stronger sentiments of friendship, than those in the middle and higher ranks. But this is what I imagine it would be difficult to prove.

These complimental phrases, which have crept into all modern languages, may, perhaps, be superfluous; or, if you please, absurd: but they are so fully established, that people of the greatest integrity must use them, both in England and in France; with this difference, that a smaller proportion will do in the language of the one country, than in that of the other; but they are indications of friendship in neither.

Friendship is a plant of slow growth, in every climate. Happy the man who can rear a few, even where he has the most settled residence. Travellers, passing through foreign countries, seldom take time to cultivate them; if they be presented with some flowers, although of a flimsy texture and quicker growth, they ought to accept of them with thankfulness, and not quarrel with the natives, for choosing to retain the other more valuable plant for their own use.

Of all travellers, the young English nobility and gentry have the least right to find fault with their entertainment while on their tours abroad; for such of them as show a desire of forming a connection with the inhabitants, by even a moderate degree of attention, are received upon easier terms than the travellers from any other country. But a very considerable number of our countrymen have not the smallest desire of that nature: they seem rather to avoid their society, and accept with reluctance every offer of hospitality. This happens partly from a prejudice against foreigners of every kind; partly from timidity or natural reserve; and in a great measure from indolence, and an absolute detestation of ceremony and restraint. Besides, they hate to be obliged to speak a language of which they seldom acquire a perfect command.

They frequently, therefore, form societies or clubs of their own, where all ceremony is dismissed, and the greatest ease and latitude allowed in behaviour, dress, and conversation. There they confirm each other in all their prejudices, and with united voice condemn and ridicule the customs and manners of every country but their own.

By this conduct the true purpose of travelling is lost or perverted; and many English travellers remain four or five years abroad, and have seldom, during all this space, been in any company but that of their own countrymen.

To go to France and Italy, and there converse with none but English people, and merely that you may have it to say that you have been in those countries, is certainly absurd: Nothing can be more so, except to adopt with enthusiasm the fashions, fopperies, taste, and manners of those countries, and transplant them to England, where they never will thrive, and where they always appear aukward and unnatural. For after all his efforts of imitation, a travelled Englishman is as different from a Frenchman or an Italian, as an English mastiff is from a monkey or a fox: And if ever that sedate and plain meaning dog should pretend to the gay friskiness of the one, or to the subtilty of the other, we should certainly value him much less than we do.

But I do not imagine that this extreme is by any means so common as the former. It is much more natural to the English character to despise foreigners than to imitate them. A few tawdry examples to the contrary, who return every winter from the continent, are hardly worth mentioning as exceptions.

LETTER XI.

Paris.

Your acquaintance B—— has been in Paris for these three weeks past. I cannot conceive how he has remained so long; for he has a very bad opinion of this nation, and is fraught with the strongest prejudice against French manners in general: He considers all their politesse as impertinence, and receives their civilities as a prelude to the picking of his pocket.

He and I went this forenoon to a review of the foot-guards, by Marshal Biron. There was a crowd; and we could with difficulty get within the circle so as to see conveniently. An old officer of high rank touched some people who stood before us, saying,—Ces deux Messieurs sont des étrangers; upon which they immediately made way, and allowed us to pass.—Don't you think that was very obliging? said I.—Yes, answered he; but, by heavens, it was very unjust.

We returned by the Boulevards, where crowds of citizens, in their holiday dresses, were making merry; the young dancing cotillons, the old beating time to the music, and applauding the dancers, all in a careless oblivion of the past, thoughtless of the future, and totally occupied with the present.—These people seem very happy, said I.—Happy! exclaimed B——; if they had common sense or reflection, they would be miserable. Why so?—Could not the minister, answered he, pick out half a dozen of them, if he pleased, and clap them into the Bicetre?—That is true indeed, said I; that is a catastrophe which, to be sure, may very probably happen, and yet I thought no more of it than they.

We met, a few days after he arrived, at a French house where we had both been invited to dinner. There was an old lady of quality present, next to whom a young officer was seated, who paid her the utmost attention.—He helped her to the dishes she liked, filled her glass with wine or water, and addressed his discourse particularly to her.—What a fool, says B——, does that young fellow make of the poor old woman! If she were my mother, d—n me, if I would not call him to an account for it.—

Though B—— understands French, and speaks it better than most Englishmen, he had no relish for the conversation, soon left the company, and has refused all invitations to dinner ever since. He generally finds some of our countrymen who dine and pass the evening with him at the Parc Royal.

After the review this day, we continued together, and being both disengaged, I proposed, by way of variety, to dine at the public ordinary of the Hôtel de Bourbon. He did not like this much at first.—I shall be teased, says he, with their confounded ceremony:—But on my observing, that we could not expect much ceremony or politeness at a public ordinary, he agreed to go.

Our entertainment turned out different, however, from my expectations and his wishes: A marked attention was paid us the moment we entered; every body seemed inclined to accommodate us with the best places. They helped us first, and all the company seemed ready to sacrifice every little conveniency and distinction to the strangers: For, next to that of a lady, the most respected character at Paris is that of a stranger.

After dinner, B—— and I walked into the gardens of the Palais Royal.

There was nothing real in all the fuss those people made about us, says he.

I can't help thinking it something, said I, to be treated with civility and apparent kindness in a foreign country—by strangers who know nothing about us, but that we are Englishmen, and often their enemies.

But their politeness consists in trifles, said he.—In what consists any body's politeness? rejoined I.—The utmost a Frenchman will do for you, added he, is to endeavour to amuse you, and make your time pass agreeably while you remain in his country. And I think that no trifle, answered I.—There are so many sources of uneasiness and vexation in this life, that I cannot help having a good will, and even gratitude, to all those who enable me to forget them:—For such people alleviate my pain, and contribute to my happiness.

But these Frenchmen, rejoined he, do not care a farthing for you in their hearts.—And why should I care a farthing for that? said I.—We have nothing to do with their hearts.—You do not expect a friend in every agreeable acquaintance.

But they are an interested set of people; and even those among them who pretend to be your friends,—do it only for some selfish end.

That is only an assertion, said I, but no proof.—If you stood in need of pecuniary assistance, they would not advance you a louis to save you from a jail, continued he.

I hope never to be perfectly convinced of that, said I;—but if we were to cultivate friendship from the idea of assistance of that nature, it would be doing exactly what you accuse them of: Besides, continued I, the power and opportunity of obliging our acquaintances and friends by great, and, what are called, essential services, seldom occur; but those attentions and courtesies, which smooth the commerce between man and man, and sweeten social life, are in every body's power, and there are daily and hourly occasions of displaying them,—particularly to strangers.—Curse their courtesies, said he, they are the greatest *Bore* in nature.—I hate the French.—They are the enemies of England, and a false, deceitful, perfidious—But as we did not come over, interrupted I, to fight them at present, we shall suspend hostilities till a more convenient season; and in the mean time, if you have no objection, let us go to the play.

He agreed to this proposal, and here our conversation ended.

You know B—— is as worthy a fellow as lives; and, under a rough address, conceals the best disposition in the world. His manner, I imagine, was originally assumed from a notion, which he has in common with many people, that great politeness, and apparent gentleness of behaviour, are generally accompanied with falsehood and real coldness;—even inhumanity of character,—as if human nature, like marble, took a polish proportionable to its hardness.

This idea is certainly formed without an accurate examination, and from a superficial view of mankind. As a boorish address is no proof of honesty, so is politeness no indication of the reverse;—and if they are once reduced to an equality in this particular, it is evident that the latter is preferable in every other respect.

But to return to the French; I am clearly of opinion, that a stranger may fairly avail himself of every conveniency arising from their obliging manners, although he should be convinced that all their assiduity and attention are unconnected with any regard to him, and flow entirely from vanity and self-love. He may perceive that his Parisian friend, while he loads him with civilities, is making a display of his own proficiency in the science of politeness, and endeavouring to thrust himself forward in the good opinion of the company, by yielding the preference on a thousand trifling occasions.—Though he plainly sees, that all this stooping is with a view to conquer, why should he repine at a victory which is accompanied with so many conveniencies to himself? why quarrel with the motive while he feels the benefit of the effect?

If writers or preachers of morality could, by the force of eloquence, eradicate selfishness from the hearts of men, and make them in reality love their neighbours as themselves, it would be a change devoutly to be wished. But until that blessed event, let us not find fault with those forms and attentions which create a kind of artificial friendship and benevolence, which for many of the purposes of society produce the same effects as the true.

People who love to amuse themselves with play, and have not ready money, are obliged to use counters. You and I, my friend, as long as we cut and shuffle together, shall never have occasion for such a succedaneum;—I am fully persuaded we are provided, on both sides, with a sufficient quantity of pure gold.

LETTER XII.

Paris.

When B—— and I went to the playhouse, as was mentioned in my last, we found a prodigious crowd of people before the door: We could not get a place till after a considerable struggle. The play was the Siege of Calais, founded on a popular story, which must needs be interesting and flattering to the French nation.

You cannot conceive what pressing and crowding there is every night to see this favourite piece, which has had the same success at Versailles as at Paris.

There are some few critics, however, who assert that it is entirely devoid of merit and owes its run to the popular nature of the subject, more than to any intrinsic beauty in the verses, which some declare are not even good French.

When it was last acted before the King, it is said, his Majesty, observing that the Duc d'Ayen did not join in applauding, but that he rather shewed some marks of disgust, turned to the Duke and said, Vous n'applaudissez pas? Vous n'étes pas bon François, Monsieur le Duc:—To this the Duke replied,—à Dieu ne plaise que je ne fusse pas meilleur que les vers de la piéce.

Obedient to the court in every other particular, the French disregard the decisions pronounced at Versailles in matters of taste. It very often happens that a dramatic piece, which has been acted before the royal family and the court, with the highest applause, is afterwards damned with every circumstance of ignominy at Paris. In all works of genius the Parisians lead the judgment of the courtiers, and dictate to their monarch.

In other countries of Europe, it has happened, that some Prince of superior talents has, by the brightness of his own genius, enlightened the minds of his subjects, and dispelled the clouds of barbarism from his dominions.

Since the commencement of this century a great empire has been improved from a state of gross ignorance, refined by the arts of peace, and instructed in the arts of war, by the vast genius and industry of one of its Princes, who laid the foundation of its present power and grandeur.

Another inconsiderable state, with fewer resources, has, at a later period, been created a powerful monarchy, by the astonishing efforts, perseverance, and magnanimity of its present king; whose love of knowledge and the arts has drawn some of the greatest geniuses in Europe to his capital; whence science and taste must gradually flow through his whole dominions, where they were formerly but little cherished.

In these instances, and others which might be enumerated, the princes have been superior in genius to any of their subjects. The throne has been the source whence knowledge and refinement have flowed to the extremities of the nation.

But this has never been the case in France, where it is not the king who polishes the people;—but the people who refine the manners, humanize the heart, and, if it be not perfectly opaque, enlighten the understanding of the king.

Telemaque, and many other works, have been composed with this intention. In many addresses and remonstrances to the throne, excellent precepts and hints are insinuated in an indirect and delicate manner.

By the emphatic applause they bestow on particular passages of the pieces represented at the theatre, they convey to the monarch the sentiments of the nation respecting the measures of his government.

By ascribing qualities to him which he does not possess, they endeavour to excite within his breast a desire to attain them: they try to cajole him into virtue. Considered in this point of view, the design of the equestrian statue which the city of Paris has erected in honour of Lewis XV. may have been suggested from a more generous motive than flattery, to which it is generally imputed. This was begun by Bouchardon; who died when the work was well advanced, and has since been committed to Pigal to be finished.

The horse is placed on a very high pedestal. At the angles, are four figures, standing in the manner of Caryatides, who represent the four virtues, Fortitude, Justice, Prudence, and the love of Peace. All the ornaments are of Bronze.

The two small sides of the pedestal are ornamented with gilded laurels and inscriptions. On the front, towards the Thuilleries, is the following:

LUDOVICO XV.
OPTIMO PRINCIPI
QUOD
AD SCALDUM, MOSAM, RHENUM,
VICTOR
PACEM ARMIS
PACE
SUORUM ET EUROPÆ
FELICITATEM
QUÆSIVIT.

The large sides of the pedestal are adorned with trophies and has reliefs. One represents Lewis giving peace to Europe; the other represents him in a triumphal chariot, crowned by Victory, and conducted by Renown to a people who submit.

When we recollect that the inscription and emblems allude to the conclusion of the war before the last, and what kind of inscriptions are usually put under the statues of kings, we shall not find any thing outrageously flattering in the above; the moral of which is, that the love of peace is one of the greatest virtues a king can possess—The best moral that can be insinuated into the breast of a monarch.

In this work the horse is infinitely more admired, by sculptors and satirists, than the king. But the greatest oversight is, that the whole group, though all the figures are larger than life, have a diminutive appearance in the centre of the vast area in which they are placed.

The wits of Paris could not allow such an opportunity of indulging their vein to escape unimproved. Many epigrams are handed about.—Here are two:

Bouchardon est un animal,

Et son ouvrage fait pitié;

Il place les vices à cheval,

Et met les vertus à pied.

Voilà notre Roi comme il est à Versailles,

Sans foi, sans loi, et sans entrailles.

Both are too severe; giving the idea of wicked dispositions, and cruelty of temper, which do not belong to Lewis the Fifteenth; whose real character, in three words, is that of a good-natured, easy-tempered man, sunk in sloth and sensuality.

I have seen another inscription for the statue handed about; it is in Latin, and very short.

STATUA STATUÆ.

You may imagine that the authors of these would meet with a dreadful punishment, if they were discovered. No danger of that kind is sufficient to restrain the inhabitants of this city, from writing and spreading such pasquinades, which are greatly relished by the whole nation.

Indeed, I imagine there is more of the spirit of revenge, than of good policy, in attempting to repel such humours; which, if they did not get vent in this manner, might break out in a more dangerous shape.

Adieu.

LETTER XIII.

Paris.

I dined yesterday with an equal number of both sexes, at the Chevalier B——'s. He is F——'s very intimate friend, and has a charming house within a few leagues of Paris, which the Marquis makes full as much use of as the owner.

The Chevalier has a considerable revenue, which he spends with equal magnificence and œconomy. He has been married many years to his present lady, a most agreeable woman, with whom he possesses every thing which can make their union happy, except children. They endeavour to forget this disagreeable circumstance, by a constant succession of company; and, which is very singular here, the society entertained by the husband and wife are the same.

F——, though much younger than either, is a great favourite of both; and they are always pleased when he invites a small company of his friends to dine at their house.

The present party was proposed by Madame de M——, a rich young widow, much admired here; of whom I shall give you a glimpse, en passant—for do not imagine I undertake to describe the most undescribable of all human beings,—a fine French lady.

Madame de M—— has some wit, more beauty, and vivacity in the greatest measure:—if there were a fourth degree of comparison, I should place her vanity there. She laughs a great deal, and she is in the right; for her teeth are remarkably fine. She talks very much, and in a loud and decisive tone of voice.—This is not so judicious, because her sentiments are not so brilliant as her teeth, and her voice is rather harsh.—She is received with attention and respect every where;—that she owes to her rank.—She is liked and followed by the men; this she owes to her beauty. She is not disliked by the women, which is probably owing to her foibles.

This lady is thought to be fond of F——: so, to prevent scandal, she desired me to call at her house, and attend her to the Chevalier's.

I found her at her toilette, in consultation with a general officer and two abbés, concerning a new head-dress which she had just invented.—It was smart and fanciful; and, after a few corrections, received the sanction of all those critics. They declared it to be a valuable discovery, and foretold that it would immediately become the general mode of Paris, and do immortal honour to the genius of Madame de M——.

She wheeled from before the glass, with an air of exultation.—Allons, donc, mes enfans—à la gloire,—cried she; and was proceeding to give orders for her equipage, when a servant entered, and informed her, that Madame la Comtesse had accepted her invitation, and would certainly do herself the honour of dining with her.

I despair of giving you an idea of the sudden change which this message occasioned in the features of Madame de M———. Had she heard of the death of her father, or her only child, she could not have been more confounded.—Est il possible (said she, with an accent of despair) qu'on puisse être si bête!—The servant was called, and examined regarding the import of the answer he had brought from Madame la Comtesse.—It was even so—she was assuredly to come.—Fresh exclamations on the part of Madame de M———. Did you send to invite her for this day? said I.—Undoubtedly I did, replied Madame de M———. That could be delayed no longer.—She came to town last Sunday.—I therefore sent her the politest message in the world, begging to have the honour of her company for this day, at dinner; and behold, the horrid woman (with a rudeness, or ignorance of life without example) sends me word she will come.

It is very shocking, indeed, said I, that she should have misunderstood your kindness so prodigiously.—Is it not, said she? Could any mortal have expected so barbarous a return of civility?—She is connected with some of my relations in the country:—when she came to town, I immediately left my name with her porter.—She called next day on me—I had informed my Swiss, that I was always to be out when she came. I was denied accordingly.—Celà est tout simple, et selon les régles. The woman is twenty years older than I, and we must be insupportable to each other.—She ought to have seen, that my invitation was dictated by politeness only:—the same politeness on her part should have prompted her to send a refusal. In this manner we might have visited each other, dined and supped together, and remained on the most agreeable footing imaginable through the whole course of our lives:—but this instance of grosièreté must put an end to all connection.—Well—there is no remedy:—I must suffer purgatory for this one day. Adieu.—Present my compliments to Madame B———. Inform her of this horrid accident.

Having condoled with Madame de M——— on her unmerited misfortune, I took my leave and joined F———, to whom I recounted the sad chance which had deprived us of that lady's company.

He did not appear quite so unhappy as she had on the occasion; but he swore he was convinced that the Countess had accepted the invitation to dinner par pure malice; for, to his knowledge, she was acquainted with their party to the Chevalier B———'s, and had certainly seized that opportunity of plaguing

Madame de M———, whom she hated. Without that douceur, he imagined, the dinner would be as great a purgatory to the Countess, as it could possibly be to Madame de M———. How these affectionate friends contrived to pass their time together I know not, but we had a most agreeable party at the Chevalier's—the Marquis entertaining the company with the history of Madame M———'s misfortune, and the loving tête à tête which it had occasioned.—This he related with such sprightliness, and described his own grief and disappointment with such a flow of good humour, as in some degree indemnified the company for the lady's absence.

LETTER XIV.

Paris.

Though the gentleness of French manners qualifies in some degree the severity of the government; as I observed in a former letter, still the condition of the common people is by no means comfortable.

When we consider the prodigious resources of this kingdom; the advantages it enjoys above almost every other country in point of soil, climate, and situation; the industry and ingenuity of the inhabitants, attached by affection to their Kings, and submissive to the laws; we naturally expect that the bulk of the nation should be at their ease, and that poverty should be as little known here as in any country of Europe. I do not speak of that ideal or comparative poverty, the child of envy and covetousness, which may be felt by the richest citizens of London or Amsterdam; or of the poverty produced in capitals by gaming, luxury, and dissipation: But of that actual poverty which arises when the laborious part of a nation cannot acquire a competent share of the necessaries of life by their industry.

The two first flow from the vices and extravagance of individuals:—The other from a bad government.

Much of the first may be found in London, where more riches circulate than in any city of Europe; of the last there is little to be seen in the country of England.

The reverse of this is the case in France, where the poorest inhabitants of the capital are often in a better situation than the laborious peasant. The former, by administering to the luxuries, or by taking advantage of the follies of the great and the wealthy, may procure a tolerable livelihood, and sometimes make a fortune; while the peasant cannot, without much difficulty, earn a scanty and precarious subsistence.

To have an adequate idea of the wealth of England, we must visit the provinces, and see how the nobility, the gentry, and especially the farmers and country people in general live. The magnificence of the former, and the abundance which prevails among the latter classes, must astonish the natives of any other country in Europe.

To retain a favourable notion of the wealth of France, we must remain in the capital, or visit a few trading or manufacturing towns; but must seldom enter the chateau of the Seigneur, or the hut of the peasant. In the one, we shall find nothing but tawdry furniture, and from the other we shall be scared by penury.

A failure of crops, or a careless administration, may occasion distress and scarcity of bread among the common people at a particular time: But when there is a permanent poverty through various reigns, and for a long tract of years, among the peasantry of such a country as France; this seems to me the surest proof of a careless, and consequently an oppressive government. Yet the French very seldom complain of their government, though often of their governors; and never of the King, but always of the minister.

Although the enthusiastic affection which the people of this nation once felt for their present monarch be greatly abated, it is not annihilated. Some of the courtiers indeed, who are supposed to administer to the King's pleasures, are detested. The imprudent ostentatious luxury of the mistress, is publicly execrated; but their censure of the King, even where they think themselves quite safe, never bursts out as it would in some other nations, in violent expressions, such as, Curse his folly,—his weakness, or—his obstinacy. No: Even their censure of him is intermingled with a kind of affectionate regret.—Naturellement il est bon, they say.—And when they observe the deplorable anxiety and disgust in his countenance, which are the concomitants of a constitution jaded by pleasure, and of a mind incapable of application, they cry, Mon Dieu, qu'il est triste!—Il est malheureux lui-même;—comment peut il penser à nous autres?

I am persuaded, that, in spite of the discontent which really subsists at present in France, the King might recover the esteem and affection of his subjects at once by the simple manœuvre of dismissing his minister, and a few other unpopular characters. A Lettre de cachet, ordering them to banishment, or shutting them up in the Bastille, would be considered as a complete *revolution* of government, and the nation would require no other *Bill of Rights* than, what proceeded from this dreadful instrument of tyranny.

As matters are at present, in my opinion, no body of men in France has, properly speaking, any rights. The Princes, the noblesse, and the clergy, have indeed certain privileges which distinguish them in different degrees from their fellow-subjects: but as for rights, they have none; or, which amounts to the same thing, none which can defend them, or which they can defend against the Monarch, whenever he in his royal wisdom chooses to invade or annihilate them.

A Frenchman will tell you, that their parliaments have the right of remonstrating to the throne upon certain occasions.—This is a precious privilege indeed! the common-council of London are in possession of this glorious right also, and we all know what it avails. It is like the power of which Owen Glendower boasted—"calling spirits from the vasty deep."—But the misfortune was, that none came in consequence of his call.

The parliaments of Paris can indeed remonstrate; and have done it with such strength of reasoning and energy of expression, that if eloquence were able to prevail over unlimited power, every grievance would have been redressed.

Some of these remonstrances display not only examples of the most sublime and pathetic eloquence, but also breathe a spirit of freedom which would do honour to a British House of Commons.

The resistance which the members of the parliament of Paris made to the will of the King, does them the greatest honour. Indeed the lawyers in France have displayed more just and manly sentiments of government, and have made a nobler struggle against despotic power, than any set of men in the kingdom. It has therefore often affected me with surprise and indignation, to observe the attempts that are made here to turn this body of men into ridicule.

One of this profession is never introduced on the stage but in a ridiculous character. This may give satisfaction to the prince, whose power they have endeavoured to limit, or to thoughtless slavish courtiers; but ought to be viewed with horror by the nation, for whose good the gentlemen of the long-robe have hazarded so much; for in their opposition to the court, much personal danger was to be feared, and no lucrative advantage to be reaped.

Those who oppose the court measures in our island incur, I thank Heaven, no personal risk on that account.—A member of the British parliament may launch his patriotic bark in the most perfect security:—He may glide down the current of inventive, spread all his canvas, catch every gale, and sail for an hour or two upon the edge of treason, without any risk of being sucked into its whirlpool. But though he has nothing to fear, it is equally evident that he has nothing to hope from such a voyage. Opposition was formerly considered as a means of getting into power: Mais nous avons changé tout cela. Let any one recollect the numbers who, with very moderate abilities, have crawled on their knees into office, and compare them with the numbers and success of those who, armed with genius and the artillery of eloquence, attempt the places by storm; if, after this, he joins the assailants, he must either act from other motives than those of self-interest, or betray his ignorance in the calculation of chances.

The security, and even the existence, of the parliament of Paris, depending entirely on the pleasure of the King, and having no other weapons, offensive or defensive, but justice, argument, and reason, their fate might have been foreseen—the usual fate of those who have no other artillery to oppose to power:—The members were disgraced, and the parliament abolished. The measure was considered as violent; the exiles were regarded as martyrs; the people were astonished and grieved. At length, recovering from their surprise, they dissipated their sorrow, as they do on all occasions of great calamity,—by some very merry songs.

LETTER XV.

Paris.

My friend F—— called on me a few days since, and as soon as he understood that I had no particular engagement, he insisted that I should drive somewhere into the country, dine tête-à-tête with him, and return in time for the play.

When we had drove a few miles I perceived a genteel-looking young fellow, dressed in an old uniform. He sat under a tree, on the grass, at a little distance from the road, and amused himself by playing on the violin. As we came nearer we perceived he had a wooden leg, part of which lay in fragments by his side.

What do you there, soldier? said the Marquis.—I am on my way home to my own village, mon officier, said the soldier.—But, my poor friend, resumed the Marquis, you will be a furious long time before you arrive at your journey's end, if you have no other carriage besides these, pointing at the fragments of his wooden leg.—I wait for my equipage and all my suite, said the soldier; and I am greatly mistaken if I do not see them this moment coming down the hill.

We saw a kind of cart, drawn by one horse, in which was a woman, and a peasant who drove the horse.—While they drew near, the soldier told us he had been wounded in Corsica—that his leg had been cut off—that before setting out on that expedition, he had been contracted to a young woman in the neighbourhood—that the marriage had been postponed till his return;—but when he appeared with a wooden leg, that all the girl's relations had opposed the match.—The girl's mother, who was her only surviving parent, when he began his courtship, had always been his friend; but she had died while he was abroad.—The young woman herself, however, remained constant in her affections, received him with open arms, and had agreed to leave her relations, and accompany him to Paris, from whence they intended to set out in the diligence to the town where he was born, and where his father still lived:—That on the way to Paris his wooden leg had snapped; which had obliged his mistress to leave him, and go to the next village in quest of a cart to carry him thither, where he would remain till such time as the carpenter should renew his leg.—C'est un malheur, mon officier, concluded the soldier, qui sera bientôt réparé—et voici mon amie!—

The girl sprang before the cart, seized the outstretched hand of her lover, and told him with a smile full of affection,—that she had seen an admirable carpenter, who had promised to make a leg that would not break, that it would be ready by the morrow, and they might resume their journey as soon after as they pleased.

The soldier received his mistress's compliment as it deserved.

She seemed about twenty years of age, a beautiful, fine-shaped girl—a Brunette, whose countenance indicated sentiment and vivacity.

You must be much fatigued, my dear, said the Marquis.—On ne se fatigue pas, Monsieur, quand on travaille pour ce qu'on aime, replied the girl.—The soldier kissed her hand with a gallant and tender air.—When a woman has fixed her heart upon a man, you see, said the Marquis, turning to me, it is not a leg more or less that will make her change her sentiments.—Nor was it his legs, said Fanchon, which made any impression on my heart. If they had made a little, however, said the Marquis, you would not have been singular in your way of thinking; but, allons, continued he, addressing himself to me.—This girl is quite charming—her lover has the appearance of a brave fellow;—they have but three legs betwixt them, and we have four;—if you have no objection, they shall have the carriage, and we will follow on foot to the next village, and see what can be done for these lovers.—I never agreed to a proposal with more pleasure in my life.

The soldier began to make difficulties about entering into the vis-à-vis.—Come, come, friend, said the Marquis, I am a Colonel, and it is your duty to obey: Get in without much ado, and your mistress shall follow.

Entrons, mon bon ami, said the girl, since these gentlemen insist upon doing us so much honour.

A girl like you would do honour to the finest coach in France. Nothing could please me more than to have it in my power to make you happy, said the Marquis,—Laisez moi faire, mon Colonel, said the soldier. Je suis heureuse comme une reine, said Fanchon.—Away moved the chaise, and the Marquis and I followed.

Voyez vous, combien nous sommes heureux nous autres François à bon marché, said the Marquis to me, adding with a smile, le bonheur, à ce qu'on m'a dit, est plus cher en Angleterre. But answered I, how long will this last with these poor people?—Ah, pour le coup, said he, voilà une reflexion bien Angloise—that, indeed, is what I cannot tell; neither do I know how long you or I may live; but I fancy it would be great folly to be sorrowful through life, because we do not know how soon misfortunes may come, and because we are quite certain that death is to come at last.

When we arrived at the inn to which we had ordered the postilion to drive, we found the soldier and Fanchon. After having ordered some victuals and wine—Pray, said I to the soldier, how do you propose to maintain your wife and yourself?—One who has contrived to live for five years on soldier's pay, replied he, can have little difficulty for the rest of his life.—I can play tolerably well on the fiddle, added he, and perhaps there is not a village in all France of the size, where there are so many marriages as in that in which we are going to settle—I shall never want employment.—And I, said Fanchon, can weave hair nets and silk purses, and mend stockings. Besides, my uncle has two hundred livres of mine in his hands, and although he is brother-in-law to the Bailiff, and *volontiers brutal*, yet I will make him pay it every sou.—And I, said the soldier, have fifteen livres in my pocket; besides two louis that I lent to a poor farmer to enable him to pay the taxes, and which he will repay me when he is able.

You see, Sir, said Fanchon to me, that we are not objects of compassion.—May we not be happy, my good friend (turning to her lover with a look of exquisite tenderness), if it be not our own fault?—If you are not, ma douce amie! said the soldier with great warmth, je ferai bien à plaindre.—I never felt a more charming sensation.—The tear trembled in the Marquis's eye.—Ma foi, said he to me, c'est une comédie larmoyante—Then, turning to Fanchon, Come hither, my dear, said he, till such time as you can get payment of the two hundred livres, and my friend here recovers his two louis, accept of this from me, putting a purse of louis into her hand—I hope you will continue to love your husband, and to be loved by him.—Let me know from time to time how your affairs go on, and how I can serve you. This will inform you of my name, and where I live. But if ever you do me the pleasure of calling at my house at Paris,—be sure to bring your husband with you; for I would not wish to esteem you less or love you more than I do this moment. Let me see you sometimes; but always bring your husband along with you.—I shall never be afraid to trust her with you, said the soldier:—She shall see you as often as she pleases, without my going with her.

It was by too much venturing (as your serjeant told me) that you lost your leg, my best friend, said Fanchon, with a smile, to her lover. Monsieur le Colonel n'est que trop aimable. I shall follow his advice literally, and when I have the honour of waiting on him, you shall always attend me.

Heaven bless you both, my good friends, said the Marquis; may he never know what happiness is who attempts to interrupt your felicity!—It shall be my business to find out some employment for you, my fellow-soldier, more profitable than playing on the fiddle. In the mean time, stay here till a coach comes, which shall bring you both this night to Paris; my servant shall provide lodgings for you, and the best surgeon for wooden legs that can be found. When you are properly equipped, let me see you before you go home. Adieu, my honest fellow; be kind to Fanchon; She seems to deserve your love. Adieu, Fanchon; I shall be happy to hear that you are as fond of Dubois two years hence as you are at present. So saying, he shook Dubois by the hand, saluted Fanchon, pushed me into the carriage before him, and away we drove.

As we returned to town, he broke out several times into warm praises of Fanchon's beauty, which inspired me with some suspicion that he might have further views upon her.

I was sufficiently acquainted with his free manner of life, and I had a little before seen him on the point of being married to one woman, after he had arranged every thing, as he called it, with another.

To satisfy myself in this particular, I questioned him in a jocular style on this subject.

No, my friend, said he, Fanchon shall never be attempted by me.—Though I think her exceedingly pretty, and of that kind of beauty too that is most to my taste; yet I am more charmed with her constancy to honest Dubois, than with any other thing about her: If she loses that, she will lose her greatest beauty in my eyes. Had she been shackled to a morose, exhausted, jealous fellow, and desired a redress of grievances, the case would have been different; but her heart is fixed upon her old lover Dubois, who seems to be a worthy man, and I dare say will make her happy. If I were inclined to try her, very probably it would be in vain:—The constancy which has stood firm against absence, and a cannon-ball, would not be overturned by the airs, the tinsel, and the jargon of a petit-maître.—It gives me pleasure to believe it would not, and I am determined never to make the trial.

F—— never appeared so perfectly amiable.

B—— called and supped with me the same evening. I was too full of the adventure of Fanchon and Dubois not to mention it to him, with all the particulars of the Marquis's behaviour.—This F—— of yours, said he, is an honest fellow. Do—contrive to let us dine with him to-morrow.—By the bye, continued he after a little pause, are not those F——'s originally from England?—I think I have heard of such a name in Yorkshire.

Adieu.

LETTER XVI.

Paris.

I am uneasy when I hear people assert, that mankind always act from motives of self-interest. It creates a suspicion that those who maintain this system, judge of others by their own feelings. This conclusion, however, may be as erroneous as the general assertion; for I have heard it maintained (perhaps from affectation) by very disinterested people, who, when pushed, could not support their argument without perverting the received meaning of language.—Those who perform generous or apparently disinterested actions, say they, are prompted by selfish motives—by the pleasure which they themselves feel.—There are people who have this feeling so strong, that they cannot pass a miserable object without endeavouring to assist him.—Such people really relieve themselves when they relieve the wretched.

All this is very true: but is it not a strange assertion, that people are not benevolent, because they cannot be otherwise?

Two men are standing near a fruit-shop in St. James's street. There are some pine-apples within the window, and a poor woman, with an infant crying at her empty breast, without. One of the gentlemen walks in, pays a guinea for a pine-apple, which he calmly devours; while the woman implores him for a penny, to buy her a morsel of bread—and implores in vain: not that this fine gentleman values a penny; but to put his hand in his pocket would give him some trouble;—the distress of the woman gives him none. The other man happens to have a guinea in his pocket also; he gives it to the woman, walks home, and dines on beef-steaks, with his wife and children.

Without doing injustice to the taste of the former, we may believe, that the latter received the greater gratification for his guinea.—You will never convince me, however, that his motive in bestowing it was as selfish as the other's.

Some few days after the adventure I mentioned in my last letter, I met F—— and B—— at the opera. They had become acquainted with each other at my lodgings two days before, according to B——'s desire.—It gave me pleasure to see them on so good a footing.

F—— invited us to go home and sit an hour with him before we went to bed;—to which we assented.

The Marquis then told us, we should have the pleasure of seeing Fanchon, in her best gown, and Dubois, with his new leg—for he had ordered his valet to invite them, with two or three of his companions, to a little supper.

While the Marquis was speaking, his coach drove up to the door of the opera—where a well-known lady was at that moment waiting for her carriage.

B—— seemed to recollect himself of a sudden, saying, he must be excused from going with us, having an affair of some importance to transact at home.

The Marquis smiled—shook B—— by the hand—saying, c'est apparemment quelque affaire qui regarde la constitution, vivent les Anglois pour l'amour patriotique.

When we arrived at the Marquis's, the servants and their guests were assembled in the little garden behind the hotel, and dancing, by moon-light, to Dubois's music.

He and Fanchon were invited to a glass of wine in the Marquis's parlour.—The poor fellow's heart swelled at the sight of his benefactor.—He attempted to express his gratitude; but his voice failed, and he could not articulate a word.

Vous n'avez pas à faire a des ingrats, Monsieur le Colonel, said Fanchon. My husband, continued she, is more affected with your goodness, that he was by the loss of his leg, or the cruelty of my relations.—She then, in a serious manner, with the voice of gratitude, and in the language of Nature, expressed her own and her husband's obligations to the Marquis; and, amongst others, she alluded to twenty louis which her husband had received *de sa part* that very afternoon.—You intend to make a saint of a sinner, my dear, said the Marquis, and to succeed the better, you invent false miracles. I know nothing of the twenty louis you mention.—But I know a great deal; for here they are in my pocket, says Dubois.—The Marquis still insisted they had not come from him. The soldier then declared, that he had called about one o'clock, to pay his duty to Monsieur de F——; but not finding him at home, he was returning to his lodgings, when, in the street, he observed a gentleman looking at him with attention, who soon accosted him, demanding if his name was not Dubois? If he had not lost his leg at Corsica? and several other questions, which being answered in the affirmative, he slipped twenty louis into his hand, telling him that it would help to furnish his house.—Dubois in astonishment had exclaimed—Mon Dieu! voilà encore Monsieur de F——. Upon which the stranger had replied:—Yes, he sends you that, by me: and immediately he turned into another street, and Dubois saw no more of him.

We were all equally surprised at the singularity of this little adventure. On enquiring more particularly about the appearance of the stranger, I was convinced he could be no other than B——.

I remembered he had been affected with the story of Dubois when I told it him. You know B—— is not one of those, who allow any emotions of that nature to pass unimproved, or to evaporate in sentiment. He generally puts them to some practical use.—So having met Dubois accidentally in the street, he had made him this small present, in the manner above related; and on his understanding that Dubois and Fanchon were at F——'s, he had declined going, to avoid any explanation on the subject.

Had our friend B—— been a man of system, or much reflection, in his charity, he would have considered, that as the soldier had already been taken good care of, and was under the protection of a generous man, there was no call for his interfering in the business; and he would probably have kept his twenty guineas for some more pressing occasion.

There are men in the world (and very useful and most respectable men no doubt they are), who examine the pro's and the con's before they decide, upon the most indifferent occasion; who are directed in all their actions by propriety, and by the general received notions of duty. They weigh, in the nicest scales, every claim that an acquaintance, a relation, or a friend may have on them; and they endeavour to pay them on demand, as they would a bill of exchange. They calculate their income, and proportion every expence; and hearing it asserted every week from the pulpit, that there is exceeding good interest to be paid one time or other, for the money that is given to the poor, they risk a little every year upon that venture. Their passions, and their affairs are always in excellent order; they walk through life undisturbed by the misfortunes of others. And when they come to the end of their journey, they are decently interred in a church-yard.

There is another set of men, who never calculate; for they are generally guided by the heart, which never was taught arithmetic, and knows nothing of accounts. Their heads have scarcely a vote in the choice of their acquaintances; and without the consent of the heart, most certainly none in their friendships. They perform acts of benevolence, without recollecting that this is a duty, merely for the pleasure they afford; and perhaps forget them, as they do their own pleasures, when past.

As for little occasional charities, these are as natural to such characters as breathing; and they claim as little merit for the one as for the other, the whole seeming an affair of instinct rather than of reflection.

That the first of these two classes of men is the most useful in society; that their affairs will be conducted with most circumspection; that they will keep out of many scrapes and difficulties that the others may fall into; and that they are (if you insist upon it very violently) the most virtuous of the two, I shall not dispute: Yet for the soul of me I cannot help preferring the other; for almost all the friends I have ever had in my life, are of the second class.

LETTER XVII.

Paris.

Considering the natural gaiety and volatility of the French nation, I have often been surprised at their fondness for tragedy, especially as their tragedies are barren of incident, full of long dialogues, and declamatory speeches;— and modelled according to the strictest code of critical legislation.

The most sprightly and fashionable people of both sexes flock to these entertainments in preference to all others, and listen with unrelaxed gravity and attention. One would imagine that such a serious, correct and uniform amusement, would be more congenial with the phlegm, and saturnine dispositions of the English, than with the gay, volatile temper of the French.

An English audience loves show, bustle and incident, in their tragedies; and have a mortal aversion to long dialogues and speeches, however fine the sentiments, and however beautiful the language may be.

In this it would seem, that the two nations had changed characters. Perhaps it would be difficult to account for it in a satisfactory manner. I shall not attempt it. A Frenchman would cut the matter short, by saying, that the Paris audience has a more correct and just taste than that of London; that the one could be amused and delighted with poetry and sentiment, while the other could not be kept awake without bustle, guards, processions, trumpets, fighting, and murder.

For my own part, I admire the French Melpomene more in the closet than on the stage. I cannot be reconciled to the French actors of tragedy. Their pompous manner of declaiming seems to me very unnatural. The strut, and superb gestures, and what they call la manière noble, of their boasted Le Kain, appear, in my eyes, a little outrè.

The justness, the dignified simplicity, the energy of Garrick's action, have destroyed my relish for any manner different from his. That exquisite, but concealed art, that magic power, by which he could melt, freeze, terrify the soul, and command the obedient passions as he pleased, we look for in vain, upon our own, or any other stage.

What Horace said of Nature, may be applied with equal justice to that unrivalled actor:

——Juvat, aut impellit ad iram,

Aut ad humum mœrore gravi deducit, et angit.

One of the most difficult things in acting is the player's concealing himself behind the character he assumes: The instant the spectator gets a peep of him, the whole illusion vanishes, and the pleasure is succeeded by disgust. In Oedipus, Mahomet, and Orosmane, I have always detected Le Kain; but I have seen the English Roscius represent Hamlet, Lear, Richard, without recollecting that there was such a person as David Garrick in the world.

The French tragedians are apt in my opinion *to overstep the modesty of nature*. Nature is not the criterion by which their merit is to be tried.—The audience measures them by a more sublime standard, and if they come not up to that, they cannot pass muster.

Natural action, and a natural elocution, they seem to think incompatible with dignity, and imagine that the hero must announce the greatness of his soul by supercilious looks, haughty gestures, and a hollow sounding voice. Such easy familiar dialogue as Hamlet holds with his old school-fellow Horatio, appears to them low, vulgar, and inconsistent with the dignity of tragedy.

But if simplicity of manners be not inconsistent in real life, with genius, and the most exalted greatness of mind, I do not see why the actor who represents a hero, should assume gestures which we have no reason to think were ever in use in any age, or among any rank of men.

Simplicity of manners, however, is so far from being inconsistent with magnanimity, that the one for the most part accompanies the other. The French have some reason to lean to this opinion; for two of the greatest men their nation ever produced were remarkable for the simplicity of their manners. Henry IV. and Maréchal Turenne were distinguished by that, as well as by their magnanimity and other heroic virtues.

How infinitely superior in real greatness and intrinsic merit, were those men to the strutting ostentatious Lewis, who was always affecting a greatness he never possessed,—till misfortune humbled his mind to the standard of humanity? Then indeed, throwing away his pageantry and bluster, he assumed true dignity, and for the first time obtained the admiration of the judicious. In the correspondence with de Torcy, Lewis's letters, which it is now certain were written and composed by himself, prove this, and display a soundness of judgement and real greatness of mind which seldom appeared in the meridian of what they call his glory.

What Lewis was (in the height of his prosperity) to Henry in the essential qualities of a King and Hero, such is Le Kain to Garrick as an actor.

The French stage can boast at present of more than one actress who may dispute the laurel of tragedy with Mrs. Yates, or Mrs. Barry.

In comedy, the French actors excel, and can produce at all times a greater number far above mediocrity, than are to be found on the English stage.

The national character and manners of the French give them perhaps advantages in this line; and besides, they have more numerous resources to supply them with actors of every kind. In all the large trading and manufacturing towns, of which there are a great number in France, there are playhouses established. The same thing takes place in most of the frontier towns, and wherever there is a garrison of two or three regiments.

There are companies of French comedians also at the northern courts, in all the large towns of Germany, and at some of the courts of Italy. All of these are academies which educate actors for the Paris stage.

In genteel comedy particularly, I imagine the French actors excel ours. They have in general more the appearance of people of fashion.

There is not such a difference between the manners and behaviour of the people of the first rank, and those of the middle and lower ranks, in France as in England. Players therefore, who wish to catch the manners of people of high rank and fashion, do not undertake so great a task in the one country as in the other.

You very seldom meet with an English servant who could pass for a man of quality or fashion; and accordingly very few people who have been in that situation ever appear on the English stage: But there are many *valets de place* in Paris so very polite, so completely possessed of all the little etiquettes, fashionable phrases, and usual airs of the *beau monde*, that if they were set off by the ornaments of dress and equipage, they would pass in many of the courts of Europe for men of fashion, très polis,—bien aimables,—tout-à-fait comme il faut, et avec infiniment d'esprit; and could be detected only at the court of France, or by such foreigners as have had opportunities of observing, and penetration to distinguish, the genuine ease, and natural politeness, which prevail among the people of rank in this country.

In the character of a lively, petulant, genteel petit-maître of fashion, Mollé excels any actor in London.

The superiority of the French in genteel comedy is still more evident with regard to the actresses. Very few English actresses have appeared equal to the parts of Lady Betty Modish, in The Careless Husband, or of Millamant, in The Way of the World. Gross absurdity, extravagant folly and affectation are easily imitated; but the elegant coquetry, the lively, playful, agreeable affectation of these two finely imagined characters, require greater powers. I imagine, however, from the execution I have observed in similar parts, that there are several actresses on the French stage at present who could do them ample justice. Except Mrs. Barry and Mrs. Abington, I know no actress in England who could give an adequate idea of all that Congreve meant in Millamant.

It is remarkable, that the latter also excels in a character the most perfectly opposite to this, that of an ill taught, aukward, country girl. Perhaps there is no such young lady in France as Congreve's Miss Prue: but if there were many such originals, no actress in that kingdom could give a copy more exquisite than Mrs. Abington's.

In low comedy the French are delightful. I can form no notion of any thing superior to Preville in many of his parts.

The little French operas which are given at the Comedie Italienne are executed in a much more agreeable manner than any thing of the same kind at London. Their ballettes also are more beautiful:—There is a gentillesse and legèreté in their manner of representing these little fanciful pieces, which make our singers and dancers appear somewhat aukward and clumsy in the companion.

As for the Italian pieces, they are now performed only thrice a week, and the French seem to have lost in a great measure their relish for them. Carlin, the celebrated Harlequin, is the only support of these pieces. You are acquainted with the wonderful naïveté and comic powers of this man, which make us forget the extravagance of the Italian drama, and which can create objects of unbounded mirth, from a chaos of the most incoherent and absurd materials.

An advantageous figure, a graceful manner, a good voice, a strong memory, an accurate judgment, are all required in a player: Sensibility, and the power of expressing the emotions of the heart by the voice and features, are indispensable. It seems therefore unreasonable, not to consider that profession as creditable, in which we expect so many qualities united; while many others are thought respectable, in which we daily see people arrive at eminence without common sense.

This prejudice is still stronger in France than in England. In a company where Mons. le Kain was, mention happened to be made, that the King of France had just granted a pension to a certain superannuated actor. An officer present, fixing his eyes on Le Kain, expressed his indignation at so much being bestowed on a rascally player, while he himself had got nothing. Eh, Monsieur! retorted the actor, comptez-vous pour rien la liberté de me parler ainsi?

LETTER XVIII.

Geneva.

I found myself so much hurried during the last week of my stay at Paris, that it was not in my power to write to you.

Ten thousand little affairs, which might have been arranged much better, and performed with more ease, had they been transacted as they occurred, were all crowded, by the slothful demon of procrastination, into the last bustling week, and executed in an imperfect manner.

I have often admired, without being able perfectly to imitate, those who have the happy talent of intermingling business with amusement.

Pleasure and business contrast and give a relish to each other, like day and night, the constant vicissitudes of which are far more delightful than an uninterrupted half year of either would be.

To pass life in the most agreeable manner, one ought not to be so much a man of pleasure as to postpone any necessary business; nor so much a man of business as to despise elegant amusement. A proper mixture of both forms a more infallible specific against *tedium* and fatigue, than a constant regimen of the most pleasant of the two.

As soon as I found the D—— of H—— disposed to leave Paris, I made the necessary arrangements for our departure, and a few days after we began our journey.

Passing through Dijon, Chalons, Macon, and a country delightful to behold, but tedious to describe, we arrived on the fourth day at Lyons.

After Paris, Lyons is the most magnificent town in France, enlivened by industry, enriched by commerce, beautified by wealth, and by its situation, in the middle of a fertile country, and at the confluence of the Saone and the Rhone. The numbers of inhabitants are estimated at 200,000. The theatre is accounted the finest in France, and all the luxuries in Paris are to be found at Lyons, though not in equal perfection.

The manners and conversation of merchants and manufacturers have been generally considered as peculiar to themselves. It is very certain that there is a striking difference in these particulars between the inhabitants of all the manufacturing and commercial towns of Britain, and those of Westminster. I could not remark the same difference between the manners and address of the people of Lyons and the courtiers of Versailles itself.

There appeared to me a wonderful similitude between the two. It is probable, however, that a Frenchman would perceive a difference where I could not. A foreigner does not observe the different accents in which an Englishman, a Scotchman, and an Irishman speak English; neither perhaps does he observe any difference between the manners and address of the inhabitants of Bristol, and those of Grosvenor-square, though all these are obvious to a native of England.

After a short stay at Lyons, we proceeded to Geneva, and here we have remained these three weeks, without feeling the smallest inclination to shift the scene. That I should wish to remain here is no way surprising, but it was hardly to be expected that the D—— of H—— would have been of the same mind.—Fortunately, however, this is the case.—I know no place on the continent to which we could go with any probability of gaining by the change: The opportunities of improvement here are many, the amusements are few in number, and of a moderate kind: The hours glide along very smoothly, and though they are not always quickened by pleasure, they are unretarded by languor and unruffled by remorse.

As for myself, I have been so very often and so miserably disappointed in my hopes of happiness by change, that I shall not, without some powerful motive, incline to forego my present state of content, for the chance of more exquisite enjoyments in a different place or situation.

I have at length learnt by my own experience (for not one in twenty profits by the experience of others), that one great source of vexation proceeds from our indulging too sanguine hopes of enjoyment from the blessings we expect, and too much indifference for those we possess. We scorn a thousand sources of satisfaction which we might have had in the interim, and permit our comfort to be disturbed, and our time to pass unenjoyed, from impatience for some imagined pleasure at a distance, which we may perhaps never obtain, or which, when obtained, may change its nature, and be no longer pleasure. Young says,

> The present moment, like a wife, we shun,
>
> And ne'er enjoy, because it is our own.

The devil thus cheats men both out of the enjoyment of this life and of that which is to come, making us in the first place prefer the pleasures of this life to those of a future state, and then continually prefer future pleasures in this life to those which are present.

The sum of all these apophthegms amounts to this:—We shall certainly remain at Geneva till we become more tired of it than at present.

LETTER XIX.

Geneva.

The situation of Geneva is in many respects as happy as the heart of man could desire, or his imagination conceive. The Rhone, rushing out of the noblest lake in Europe, flows through the middle of the city, which is encircled by fertile fields, cultivated by the industry, and adorned by the riches and taste, of the inhabitants.

The long ridge of mountains called Mount Jura on the one side, with the Alps, the Glaciers of Savoy, and the snowy head of Mont Blanc on the other, serve as boundaries to the most charmingly variegated landscape that ever delighted the eye.

With these advantages in point of situation, the citizens of Geneva enjoy freedom untainted by licentiousness, and security unbought by the horrors of wars.

The great number of men of letters, who either are natives of the place, or have chosen it for their residence, the decent manners, the easy circumstances, and humane dispositions of the Genevois in general, render this city and its environs a very desirable retreat for people of a philosophic turn of mind, who are contented with moderate and calm enjoyments, have no local attachments or domestic reasons for preferring another country, and who wish in a certain degree to retire from the bustle of the world, to a narrower and calmer scene, and there for the rest of their days—

 Ducere solicitæ jucunda oblivia vitæ.

As education here is equally cheap and liberal, the citizens of Geneva of both sexes are remarkably well instructed. I do not imagine that any country in the world can produce an equal number of persons (taken without election from all degrees and professions) with minds so much cultivated as the inhabitants of Geneva possess.

It is not uncommon to find mechanics in the intervals of their labour amusing themselves with the works of Locke, Montesquieu, Newton, and other productions of the same kind.

When I speak of the cheapness of a liberal education, I mean for the natives and citizens only; for strangers now find every thing dear at Geneva. Wherever Englishmen resort, this is the case. If they do not find things dear, they soon make them so.

The democratical nature of their government inspires every citizen with an idea of his own importance: He perceives that no man in the republic can insult, or even neglect him, with impunity.

It is an excellent circumstance in any government, when the most powerful man in the state has something to fear from the most feeble. This is the case here: The meanest citizen of Geneva is possessed of certain rights, which render him an object deserving the attention of the greatest. Besides, a consciousness of this makes him respect himself; a sentiment, which, within proper bounds, has a tendency to render a man respectable to others.

The general character of human nature forbids us to expect that men will always act from motives of public spirit, without an eye to private interest. The best form of government, therefore, is that in which the interest of individuals is most intimately blended with the public good.—This may be more perfectly accomplished in a small republic than in a great monarchy.— In the first, men of genius and virtue are discovered and called to offices of trust by the impartial admiration of their fellow-citizens—in the other, the highest places are disposed of by the caprice of the prince, or of his mistress, or of those courtiers, male or female, who are nearest his person, watch the variations of his humour, and know how to seize the smiling moments, and turn them to their own advantage or that of their dependents. Montesquieu says, that a sense of honour produces the same effects in a monarchy, that public spirit or patriotism does in a republic: It must be remembered, however, that the first, according to the modern acceptation of the word, is generally confined to the nobility and gentry; whereas public spirit is a more universal principle, and spreads through all the members of the commonwealth.

As far as I can judge, a spirit of independency and freedom, tempered by sentiments of decency and the love of order, influence, in a most remarkable manner, the minds of the subjects of this happy republic.

Before I knew them, I had formed an opinion, that the people of this place were fanatical, gloomy-minded, and unsociable as the puritans in England, and the presbyterians in Scotland were, during the civil wars, and the reigns of Charles II. and his brother. In this, however, I find I had conceived a very erroneous notion.

There is not, I may venture to assert, a city in Europe where the minds of the people are less under the influence of superstition or fanatical enthusiasm than at Geneva. Servetus, were he now alive, would not run the smallest risk of persecution. The present clergy have, I am persuaded, as little the inclination as the power of molesting any person for speculative opinions.

Should the Pope himself chuse this city for a retreat, it would be his own fault if he did not live in as much security as at the Vatican.

The clergy of Geneva in general are men of sense, learning, and moderation, impressing upon the minds of their hearers the tenets of Christianity with all the graces of pulpit eloquence, and illustrating the efficacy of the doctrine by their conduct in life.

The people of every station in this place attend sermons and the public worship with remarkable punctuality. The Sunday is honoured with the most respectful decorum during the hours of divine service; but as soon as that is over, all the usual amusements commence.

The public walks are crowded by all degrees of people in their best dresses.—The different societies, and what they call circles, assemble in the houses and gardens of individuals.—They play at cards and at bowls, and have parties upon the lake with music.

There is one custom universal here, and, as far as I know, peculiar to this place: The parents form societies for their children at a very early period of their lives. These societies consist of ten, a dozen, or more children of the same sex, and nearly of the same age and situation in life. They assemble once a week in the houses of the different parents, who entertain the company by turns with tea, coffee, biscuits and fruit; and then leave the young assembly to the freedom of their own conversation.

This connection is strictly kept up through life, whatever alterations may take place in the situations or circumstances of the individuals. And although they should afterwards form new or preferable intimacies, they never entirely abandon this society; but to the latest period of their lives continue to pass a few evenings every year with the companions of their youth and their earliest friends.

The richer class of the citizens have country-houses adjacent to the town, where they pass one half of the year. These houses are all of them neat, and some of them splendid. One piece of magnificence they possess in greater perfection than the most superb villa of the greatest lord in any other part of the world can boast, I mean the prospect which almost all of them command.—The gardens and vineyards of the republic,—the Païs de Vaux;—Geneva with its lake;—innumerable country-seats;—castles, and little towns around the lake;—the vallies of Savoy, and the loftiest mountains of the Alps, all within one sweep of the eye.

Those whose fortunes or employments do not permit them to pass the summer in the country, make frequent parties of pleasure upon the lake, and dine and spend the evening at some of the villages in the environs, where they amuse themselves with music and dancing.

Sometimes they form themselves into circles consisting of forty or fifty persons, and purchase or hire a house and garden near the town, where they assemble every afternoon during the summer, drink coffee, lemonade, and other refreshing liquors; and amuse themselves with cards, conversation, and playing at bowls; a game very different from that which goes by the same name in England; for here, instead of a smooth level green, they often chuse the roughest and most unequal piece of ground. The player, instead of rolling the bowl, throws it in such a manner, that it rests in the place where it first touches the ground; and if that be a fortunate situation, the next player pitches his bowl directly on his adversary's, so as to make that spring away, while his own fixes itself in the spot from which the other has been dislodged.—Some of the citizens are astonishingly dexterous at this game, which is more complicated and interesting than the English manner of playing.

They generally continue these circles till the dusk of the evening, and the sound of the drum from the ramparts call them to the town; and at that time the gates are shut, after which no person can enter or go out, the officer of the guard not having the power to open them, without an order from the Syndics, which is not to be obtained but on some great emergency.

LETTER XX.

Geneva.

The mildness of the climate, the sublime beauties of the country, and the agreeable manners of the inhabitants, are not, in my opinion, the greatest attractions of this place.

Upon the same hill, in the neighbourhood of Geneva, three English families at present reside, whose society would render any country agreeable.

The house of Mr. N—— is a temple of hospitality, good humour, and friendship.

Near to him lives your acquaintance Mr. U——. He perfectly answers your description, lively, sensible, and obliging; and, I imagine, happier than ever you saw him, having since that time drawn a great prize in the matrimonial lottery.

Their nearest neighbours are the family of Mr. L——. This gentleman, his lady and children, form one of the most pleasing pictures of domestic felicity I ever beheld. He himself is a man of refined taste, a benevolent mind, and elegant manners.

These three families, who live in the greatest cordiality with the citizens of Geneva, their own countrymen, and one another, render the hill of Cologny the most delightful place perhaps at this moment in the world.

The English gentlemen, who reside in the town, often resort hither, and mix with parties of the best company of Geneva.

I am told, that our young countrymen never were on so friendly and sociable a footing with the citizens of this republic as at present, owing in a great degree to the conciliatory manners of these three families, and to the great popularity of an English nobleman, who has lived with his lady and son in this state for several years.

I formerly mentioned, that all who live in town, must return from their visits in the country at sun-set, otherwise they are certain of being shut out;—the Genevois being wonderfully jealous of the external, as well as the internal enemies of their independency. This jealousy has been transmitted from one generation to another, ever since the attempt made by the Duke of Savoy, in the year 1602, to seize upon the town.

He marched an army, in the middle of a dark night, in the time of peace, to the gates, applied scaling ladders to the ramparts and walls, and having surprised the centinels, several hundreds of the Savoyard soldiers had actually got into the town, and the rest were following, when they were at length discovered by a woman, who gave the alarm.

The Genevois started from their sleep, seized the readiest arms they could find, attacked the assailants with spirit and energy, killed numbers in the street, drove others out of the gate, or tumbled them over the ramparts, and the few who were taken prisoners, they beheaded next morning, without further process or ceremony.

The Genevois annually distinguish the day on which this memorable exploit was performed, as a day of public thanksgiving and rejoicing.

It is called le jour de l'Escalade. There is divine worship in all the churches.—The clergymen, on this occasion, after sermon, recapitulate all the circumstances of this interesting event; put the audience in mind of the gratitude they owe to Divine Providence, and to the valour of their ancestors, which saved them in so remarkable a manner from civil and religious bondage; enumerate the peculiar blessings which they enjoy; and exhort them, in the most pathetic strain, to watch over their liberties, remain steady in their religion, and transmit these, and all their other advantages, unimpaired to their posterity.

The evening of the jour de l'Escalade is spent in visiting, feasting, dancing, and all kinds of diversions; for the Genevois seldom venture on great festivity, till they have previously performed their religious duties—In this, observing the maxim of the Psalmist,—to join trembling with their mirth.

The State keeps in pay a garrison of six hundred mercenaries, who mount guard and do duty every day. But they do not trust the safety of the republic to these alone. All citizens of Geneva are soldiers. They are exercised several hours, daily, for two months, every summer; during which time they wear their uniforms, and at the end of that period are reviewed by the Syndics.

As they receive no pay, and as the officers are their fellow-citizens, it cannot be imagined that these troops will perform the manual exercise and military evolutions, with the exactness of soldiers who have no other occupation, and who are under all the rigour of military discipline.

Nevertheless they make a very respectable figure in the eyes even of disinterested spectators; who are, however, but few in number, the greater part consisting of their own parents, wives and children. So, I dare swear, there are no troops in the world, who, at a review, are beheld with more approbation than those of Geneva.

Even a stranger of a moderate share of sensibility, who recollects the connection between the troops and the beholders, who observes the anxiety, the tenderness, the exultation, and various movements of the heart, which appear in the countenances of the spectators, will find it difficult to remain unconcerned:—But sympathising with all around him, he will naturally yield to the pleasing emotions, and at length behold the militia of Geneva with the eyes of a citizen of the republic.

Geneva, like all free states, is exposed to party-rage, and the public harmony is frequently interrupted by political squabbles. Without entering into a detail of the particular disputes which agitate them at present, I shall tell you in general, that one part of the citizens are accused of a design of throwing all the power into the hands of a few families, and of establishing a complete aristocracy. The other opposes every measure which is supposed to have that tendency, and by their adversaries are accused of seditious designs.

It is difficult for strangers who reside here any considerable time, to observe a strict neutrality. The English in particular are exceedingly disposed to take part with one side or other; and as the government has not hitherto attempted to bribe them, they generally attach themselves to the opposition.

Walking one afternoon with a young nobleman, who, to a strong taste for natural philosophy, unites the most passionate zeal for civil liberty, we passed near the garden, in which one of those circles which support the pretensions of the magistracy assemble. I proposed joining them. No, said my Lord, with indignation; I will not go for a moment into such a society: I consider these men as the enemies of their country, and that place as a focus for consuming freedom.

Among the citizens themselves, political altercations are carried on with great fire and spirit. A very worthy old gentleman, in whose house I have been often entertained with great hospitality, declaiming warmly against certain measures of the council, asserted, that all those who had promoted them deserved death; and if it depended on him, they should all be hanged, without loss of time. His brother, who was in that predicament, interrupted him, and said, with a tone of voice which seemed to beg for mercy, Good God! brother! surely you would not push your resentment so far: you would not actually hang them? Oui assurément, replied the patriot, with a determined countenance, et vous, mon très cher frère, vous seriez le premier pendu pour montrer mon impartialité.

LETTER XXI.

Geneva.

Although this republic has long continued in a profound peace, and there is no great probability of its being soon engaged in bloody conflict, yet the citizens of Geneva are not the less fond of the pomp of war.

This appears in what they call their military feasts, which are their most favourite amusements, and which they take every opportunity of enjoying.

I was present lately at a very grand entertainment of this kind, which was given by the King of the Arquebusiers upon his accession to the royal dignity.

This envied rank is neither transmitted by hereditary right, nor obtained by election; but gained by skill and real merit.

A war with this state, like the war of Troy, must necessarily consist of a siege. The skilful use of the cannon and arquebuse is therefore thought to be of the greatest importance. During several months every year, a considerable number of the citizens are almost constantly employed in firing at a mark, which is placed at a proper distance.

Any citizen has a right, at a small expence, to make trial of his skill in this way; and after a due number of trials, the most expert marksman is declared King.

There has not been a coronation of this kind these ten years, his late Majesty having kept peaceable possession of the throne during that period. But this summer, Mr. Moses Maudrier was found to excel in skill every competitor; and was raised to the throne by the unanimous voice of the judges.

He was attended to his own house from the field of contest by the Syndics, amidst the acclamations of the people. Some time after this, on the day of his feast, a camp was formed on a plain, without the gates of the city.

Here the whole forces of the republic, both horse and foot, were assembled, and divided into two distinct armies. They were to perform a battle in honour of his Majesty, all the combatants having previously studied their parts.

This very ingenious, warlike drama had been composed by one of the reverend ministers, who is said to possess a very extensive military genius.

That the ladies and people of distinction, who were not to be actually engaged, might view the action with the greater ease and safety, a large amphitheatre of seats was prepared for them, at a convenient distance from the field of battle.

Every thing being in readiness, the Syndics, the Council, strangers of distinction, and the relations and favourites of the King, assembled at his Majesty's palace, which is a little snug house, situated in a narrow lane in the lower part of the city. From the palace, the procession set out in the following order:

His Majesty walked first, supported by the two eldest Syndics.

In the next rank was the Duke of H——, with the youngest.

After these, walked Lord St——pe, the Prince Gallitzen,—Mr. Cl——ve, son to Lord Cl——ve; Mr. Gr——lle, son to the late Minister; Mr. St. L——, and many other English gentlemen, who had been invited to the feast.

Next to them came the Council of twenty-five; and the procession was closed by the King's particular friends and relations.

In this order they marched through the city, preceded by a band of music, who played, as you may believe, the most martial tunes they possibly could think of.

When this company came to the field where the troops were drawn up, they were saluted by the officers; and having made a complete circuit of both armies, the King and all his attendants took their seats at the amphitheatre, which had been prepared for that purpose.

The impatience of the troops had been very visible for some time. When the King was seated, their ardour could be no longer restrained. They called loudly to their officers to lead them to glory.—The signal was given.—They advanced to the attack in the most undaunted manner.—Conscious that they fought under the eyes of their King, the Syndics, of their wives, children, mothers and grandmothers, they disdained the thoughts of retreat.—They stood undisturbed by the thickest fire. They smiled at the roaring of the cannon, and like the horse in Job, they cried among the trumpets, ha, ha!

The ingenious author of the battle had taken care to diversify it with several entertaining incidents.

An ambuscade was placed by one of the armies, behind some trees, to surprise the enemy.—This succeeded to a miracle, although the ambuscade was posted in the sight of both armies, and all the spectators.

A convoy with provisions, advancing towards one of the armies, was attacked by a detachment from the other; and after a smart skirmish, one half of the waggons were carried away by the assailants:—The other remained with the troops for whom they seemed to have been originally intended.

A wooden bridge was briskly attacked, and as resolutely defended; but at length was trod to pieces by both armies; for, in the fury of the fight, the combatants forgot whether this poor bridge was their friend or their foe. By what means it got into the midst of the battle, I never could conceive; for there was neither river, brook, nor ditch in the whole field.

The cavalry on both sides performed wonders.—It was difficult to determine which of the generals distinguished himself most. They were both dressed in clothes exuberantly covered with lace; for the sumptuary laws were suspended for this day, that the battle might be as magnificent as possible.

As neither of these gallant commanders would consent to the being defeated, the reverend author of the engagement could not make the catastrophe so decisive and affecting as he intended.

While Victory, with equipoised wings, hovered over both armies, a messenger arrived from the town-hall with intelligence that dinner was ready. This news quickly spread among the combatants, and had an effect similar to that which the Sabine women produced when they rushed between their ravishers and their relations.—The warriors of Geneva relented at once; and both armies suspended their animosity, in the contemplation of that which they both loved.—They threw down their arms, shook hands, and were friends.

Thus ended the battle.—I don't know how it will affect you; but it has fatigued me so completely, that I have lost all appetite for the feast, which must therefore be delayed till another post.

LETTER XXII.

Geneva.

The same company which had attended the King to the field of battle, marched with him in procession from that to the Maison de Ville, where a sumptuous entertainment was prepared.

This was exactly the reverse of a fête champêtre, being held in the town-house, and in the middle of the streets adjacent; where tables were covered, and dinner provided, for several hundreds of the officers and soldiers.

The King, the Syndics, most of the members of the Council, and all the strangers, dined in the town-hall. The other rooms, as well as the outer court, were likewise full of company.

There was much greater havoc at dinner than had been at the battle, and the entertainment in other respects was nearly as warlike.

A kettle-drum was placed in the middle of the hall, upon which a martial flourish was performed at every toast. This was immediately answered by the drums and trumpets without the hall, and the cannon of the bastion.

Prosperity to the republic is a favourite toast:—When this was announced by the first Syndic, all the company stood up with their swords drawn in one hand, and glasses filled with wine in the other.

Having drank the toast, they clashed their swords, a ceremony always performed in every circle or club where there is a public dinner, as often as this particular toast is named.—It is an old custom, and implies that every man is ready to fight in defence of the republic.

After we had been about two hours at table, a new ceremony took place, which I expected as little in the middle of a feast. An hundred grenadiers, with their swords drawn, marched with great solemnity into the middle of the hall, for the tables being placed in the form of a horse-shoe, there was vacant space in the middle sufficient to admit them.

They desired permission to give a toast: This being granted, each of the grenadiers, by a well-timed movement, like a motion in the exercise, pulled from his pocket a large water glass, which being immediately filled with wine, one of the soldiers, in the name of all, drank a health to King Moses the first. His example was followed by his companions and all the company, and was instantly honoured by the sound of the drums, trumpets, and artillery.

When the grenadiers had drank this, and a toast or two more, they wheeled about, and marched out of the hall with the same solemnity with which they had entered, resuming their places at the tables in the street.

Soon after this a man fantastically dressed entered the hall, and distributed among the company some printed sheets which seemed to have come directly from the press.

This proved to be a song made for the occasion, replete with gaiety, wit, and good sense, pointing out, in a humorous strain, the advantages which the citizens of Geneva possessed, and exhorting them to unanimity, industry, and public spirit.—This ditty was sung by the man who brought it, while many of the company joined in the chorus.

When we descended from the town-hall, we found the soldiers intermingled with their officers, still seated at the tables in the streets, and encircled by their wives and children.

They all arose soon after, and dividing into different companies, repaired to the ramparts, the fields, and the gardens where, with music and dancing, they continued in high glee during the rest of the evening.

The whole exhibition of the day, though no very just representation of the manœuvres of war, or the elegance of a court entertainment, formed the most lively picture of jollity, mirth, good-humour and cordiality, that I had ever seen.

The inhabitants of a whole city,—of a whole state if you please, united in one scene of good fellowship, like a single family, is surely no common sight.

If this sketch conveys one half of the satisfaction to your mind, which the scene itself afforded mine, you will not think these two long letters tedious.

LETTER XXIII.

Geneva.

There are some of the citizens of Geneva themselves who deride the little military establishment of the republic, and declare it to be highly ridiculous in such a feeble state to presume that they could defend themselves. The very idea of resistance against Savoy or France, they hold as absurd.

They seem to take pleasure in mortifying their countrymen, assuring them, that in case of an attack all their efforts would be fruitless, and their garrison unable to stand a siege of ten days.

These politicians declaim against the needless expence of keeping the fortifications in repair, and they calculate the money lost, by so many manufacturers being employed in wielding useless firelocks, instead of the tools of their respective professions.

Were I a member of this republic, I should have no patience with these discouraging malcontents, who endeavour to depress the minds of their countrymen, and embitter a source of real enjoyment.

I am convinced that the garrison, small as it is, aided by the zeal of the inhabitants, and regulated by that share of discipline which their situation admits, would be sufficient to secure them from a coup-de-main, or any immediate insult, and might enable them to defend the town from the attempts of any one of the neighbouring states, till they should receive succour from some of the others.

Independent of these considerations, the ramparts are most agreeable walks, convenient for the inhabitants, and ornamental to the city.

The exercising and reviewing the militia form an innocent and agreeable spectacle to the women and children, contribute to the health and amusement of the troops themselves, and inspire the inhabitants in general with the pleasing ideas of security and of their own importance.

Upon the whole, I am convinced that the fortifications, and the militia of Geneva, produce more happiness, in these various ways taken together, than could be purchased by all the money they cost, expended in any other manner.

This I imagine is more than can be said in favour of the greater part of the standing armies on the continent of Europe, whose numbers secure the despotism of the prince, whose maintenance is a most severe burden upon the countries which support them, and whose discipline, instead of exciting pleasing emotions, impresses the mind with horror.

The individuals who compose those armies are miserable, by the tyranny exercised on them, and are themselves the cause of misery to their fellow-citizens by the tyranny they exercise.

But it will be said they defend the nation from foreign enemies.—Alas, could a foreign conqueror occasion more wretchedness than such defenders?—When he who calls himself my protector has stripped me of my property, and deprived me of my freedom, I cannot return him very cordial thanks, when he tells me, that he will defend me from every other robber.

The most solid security which this little republic has for its independency, is founded on the mutual jealousy of its neighbours.

There is no danger of its meeting with the misfortune which has so lately befallen Poland.—Geneva is such an atom of a state as not to be divisible.

It serves, however, as a kind of barrier or alarm-post to the Swiss Cantons, particularly that of Bern, which certainly would not like to see it in the hands either of the King of France or of Sardinia.

The acquisition is not worth the attention of the first; and it is better for the second, that the republic should remain in its present free and independent situation, than that it should revert to his possession, and be subjected to the same government with his other dominions.

For no sooner would Geneva be in the possession of Sardinia, than the wealthiest of the citizens would abandon it, and carry their families and riches to Switzerland, Holland, or England.

Trade and manufactures would dwindle with the spirit and independence of the inhabitants; and the flourishing, enlightened, happy city of Geneva, like other towns of Piedmont and Savoy, would become the residence of oppression, superstition, and poverty.

In this situation it could add but little to the King's revenue; whereas, at present, the peasants of his dominions resort in great numbers to Geneva every market-day, where they find a ready sale for all the productions of their farms. The land is, on this account, more valuable, and the peasants are more at their ease, though the taxes are very high, than in any other part of Savoy.

This republic, therefore, in its present independent state, is of more use to the King of Sardinia, than if it were his property.

If a wealthy merchant should purchase a piece of ground from a poor Lord, build a large house, and form beautiful gardens upon it, keep a number of servants, spend a great part of his revenue in good housekeeping and hospitality, the consumption of his table, and many other articles, being purchased from this Lord's tenants, it is evident that they would become rich, and be able to pay a larger rent to their landlord. This Lord would certainly act against his own interest, if he attempted, by law, chicane, or force, to dispossess the proprietor of the house and gardens.

The free republic of Geneva is to the King of Sardinia, exactly what the supposed rich man would be to the poor Lord.

It affords me satisfaction to perceive, that the stability of this little fabric of freedom, raised by my friends the citizens of Geneva, does not depend on the justice and moderation of the neighbouring powers, or any equivocal support; but is founded on the solid, lasting pillars of their mutual interest.

LETTER XXIV.

Geneva.

I returned a few days since from a journey to the Glaciers of Savoy, the Pays de Vallais, and other places among the Alps.

The wonderful accounts I had heard of the Glaciers had excited my curiosity a good deal, while the air of superiority assumed by some who had made this boasted tour, piqued my pride still more.

One could hardly mention any thing curious or singular, without being told by some of those travellers, with an air of cool contempt—Dear Sir,—that is pretty well; but, take my word for it, it is nothing to the Glaciers of Savoy.

I determined at last not to take their word for it, and I found some gentlemen of the same way of thinking. The party consisted of the Duke of H——, Mr. U——, Mr. G——, Mr. K——, and myself.

We left Geneva early in the morning of the third of August, and breakfasted at Bonneville, a small town in the duchy of Savoy, situated at the foot of Mole, and on the banks of the river Arve.

The summit of Mole, as we were told, is about 4600 English feet above the lake of Geneva, at the lower passage of the Rhone, which last is about 1200 feet above the level of the Mediterranean. For these particulars, I shall take the word of my informer, whatever airs of superiority he may assume on the discovery.

From Bonneville we proceeded to Cluse, by a road tolerably good, and highly entertaining on account of the singularity and variety of landscape to be seen from it. The objects change their appearance every moment as you advance, for the path is continually winding, to humour the position of the mountains, and to gain an access between the rocks, which in some places hang over it in a very threatening manner. The mountains overlook and press so closely upon this little town of Cluse, that when I stood in the principal street, each end of it seemed to be perfectly shut up; and wherever any of the houses had fallen down, the vacancy appeared to the eye, at a moderate distance, to be plugged up in the same manner by a green mountain.

On leaving Cluse, however, we found a well-made road running along the banks of the Arve, and flanked on each side by very high hills, whose opposite sides tally so exactly, as to lead one to imagine they have been torn from each other by some violent convulsion of nature.

In other places one side of this defile is a high perpendicular rock, so very smooth that it seems not to have been torn by nature, but chiselled by art, from top to bottom, while the whole of the side directly opposite is of the most smiling verdure.

The passage between the mountains gradually opens as you advance, and the scene diversifies with a fine luxuriancy of wild landscape.

Before you enter the town of Sallenche, you must cross the Arve, which at this season is much larger than in winter, being swoln by the dissolving snows of the Alps.

This river has its source at the Parish of Argentiere, in the valley of Chamouni, is immediately augmented by torrents from the neighbouring Glaciers, and pours its chill turbid stream into the Rhone, soon after that river issues from the lake of Geneva.

The contrast between those two rivers is very striking, the one being as pure and limpid as the other is foul and muddy. The Rhone seems to scorn the alliance, and keeps as long as possible unmingled with his dirty spouse. Two miles below the place of their junction, a difference and opposition between this ill-sorted couple is still observable; these, however, gradually abate by long habit, till at last, yielding to necessity, and to those unrelenting laws which joined them together, they mix in perfect union, and flow in a common stream to the end of their course.

We passed the night at Sallenche, and the remaining part of our journey not admitting of chaises, they were sent back to Geneva, with orders to the drivers, to go round by the other side of the lake, and meet us at the village of Martigny, in the Pays de Vallais.

We agreed with a muleteer at Sallenche, who provided mules to carry us over the mountains to Martigny. It is a good day's journey from Sallenche to Chamouni, not on account of the distance, but from the difficulty and perplexity of the road, and the steep ascents and descents with which you are teased alternately the whole way.

Some of the mountains are covered with pine, oak, beech, and walnut trees. These are interspersed with apple, plum, cherry, and other fruit trees, so that we rode a great part of the forenoon in shade.

Besides the refreshing coolness this occasioned, it was most agreeable to me on another account. The road was in some places so exceedingly steep, that I never doubted but some of us were to fall; I therefore reflected with satisfaction, that those trees would probably arrest our course, and hinder us from rolling a great way.

But many pathless craggy mountains remained to be traversed after we had lost the protection of the trees. We then had nothing but the sagacity of our mules to trust to. For my own part, I was very soon convinced that it was much safer on all dubious occasions to depend on their's than on my own: For as often as I was presented with a choice of difficulties, and the mule and I were of different opinions, if, becoming more obstinate than he, I insisted on his taking my track, I never failed to repent it, and often was obliged to return to the place where the controversy had begun, and follow the path to which he had pointed at first.

It is entertaining to observe the prudence of these animals in making their way down such dangerous rocks. They sometimes put their heads over the edge of the precipice, and examine with anxious circumspection every possible way by which they can descend, and at length are sure to fix on that which upon the whole is the best. Having observed this in several instances, I laid the bridle on the neck of my mule, and allowed him to take his own way, without presuming to controul him in the smallest degree.

This is doubtless the best method, and what I recommend to all my friends in their journey through life, when they have mules for their companions.

We rested some time, during the sultry heat of the day, at a very pleasingly situated village called Serve; and ascending thence along the steepest and roughest road we had yet seen, we passed by a mountain, wherein, they told us, there is a rich vein of copper, but that the proprietors have left off working it for many years.

As we passed through one little village, I saw many peasants going into a church.—It was some Saint's day.—The poor people must have half-ruined themselves by purchasing gold-leaf.—Every thing was gilded.—The virgin was dressed in a new gown of gold paper;—the infant in her arms was equally brilliant, all but the periwig on his head, which was milk-white, and had certainly been fresh powdered that very morning.

I could scarcely refrain from smiling at this ridiculous sight, which the people beheld with as much veneration as they could have shewn, had the originals been present.

Upon calling up my eyes to the cieling, I saw something more extraordinary still: This was a portrait of God the Father, sitting on a cloud, and dressed like a Pope, with the tiara on his head. Any one must naturally be shocked at this, if he be not at the same instant moved to laughter at the infinite absurdity of the idea.

About six in the evening we arrived at the valley of Chamouni, and found lodgings in a small village called Prieuré. The valley of Chamouni is about six leagues in length, and an English mile in breadth. It is bounded on all sides by very high mountains. Between the intervals of these mountains, on one side of the valley, the vast bodies of snow and ice, which are called Glaciers, descend from mount Blanc, which is their source.

On one side of the valley, opposite to the Glaciers, stands Breven, a mountain whose ridge is 5300 English feet higher than the valley. Many travellers who have more curiosity, and who think less of fatigue than we, take their first view of the Glaciers from the top of mount Breven. As there is only the narrow valley between that and the Glaciers, all of which it overlooks, and every other object around, except Mont Blanc, the view from it must be very advantageous and magnificent.

We determined to begin with Montanvert, from which we could walk to the Glaciers, reserving Mount Breven for another day's work, if we should find ourselves so inclined. After an hour's refreshment at our quarters, Mr. K—— and I took a walk through the valley.

The chapter of Priests and Canons of Sallenche have the lordship of Chamouni, and draw a revenue from the poor inhabitants; the highest mountains of the Alps, with all their ice and snow, not being sufficient to defend them from rapacity and extortion.

The priest's house is beyond comparison the best in the whole valley. Looking at it, I asked a young man who stood near me, if the priest was rich?

Oui, Monsieur, horriblement,—replied he,—et aussi il mange presque tout notre blé.

I then asked, if the people of Chamouni wished to get rid of him?

Oui, bien de celui-ci—mais il faut avoir un autre.

I do not see the absolute necessity of that, said I.—Consider, if you had no priest, you would have more to eat.

The lad stared—then answered with great *naïveté*—Ah, Monsieur, dans ce pays-ci les prêtres sont tout aussi nécessaires que le manger.

It is plain, that this clergyman instructs his parishioners very carefully in the principles of religion.—I perceive, that your soul is in very safe hands, said

K——, giving the boy a crown; but here is something to enable you to take care of your body.

In my next I shall endeavour to give you some account of the Glaciers:—At present, I must wish you good night.

LETTER XXV.

Geneva.

We began pretty early in the morning to ascend Montanvert, from the top of which, there is easy access to the Glacier of that name, and to the valley of ice.

Our mules carried us from the inn across the valley, and even for a considerable way up the mountain; which at length became so exceedingly steep, that we were obliged to dismount and send them back, Mr. U—— only, who had been here before, and was accustomed to such expeditions, continued without compunction on his mule till he got to the top, riding fearless over rocks, which a goat or a chamois would have passed with caution.

In this last animal, which is to be found on these mountains only, are blended the different qualities of the goat and the deer.—It is said to have more agility than any other quadruped possessed of the same degree of strength.

After ascending four hours, we gained the summit of Montanvert. The day was remarkably fine, the objects around noble and majestic, but in some respects different from what I had expected.

The valley of Chamouni had disappeared:—Mount Breven seemed to have crept wonderfully near; and if I had not just crossed the plain which separates the two mountains, and is a mile in breadth, I should have concluded that their bases were in contact, and that their distance above was solely owing to the diminution in the size of all mountains towards the summit. Judging from the eye alone, I should have thought it possible to have thrown a stone from the place where I stood to Mount Breven.

There is a chain of mountains behind Montanvert, all covered with snow, which terminate in four distinct rocks, of a great height, having the appearance of narrow pyramids or spires. They are called the Needles; and each has a distinct name.—Mont Blanc, surrounded by Montanvert, Mount Breven, the Needles, and other snowy mountains, appears like a giant among pygmies.

The height which we had now attained, was so far on our way up this mountain. I was therefore equally surprised and mortified to find, after an ascent of three thousand feet, that Mont Blanc seemed as high here as when we were in the valley.

Having ascended Montanvert from Chamouni, on descending a little on the other side, we found ourselves on a plain, whose appearance has been aptly compared to that which a stormy sea would have, if it were suddenly arrested and fixed by a strong frost. This is called the Valley of Ice. It stretches several leagues behind Montanvert, and is reckoned 2300 feet higher than the valley of Chamouni.

From the highest part of Montanvert we had all the following objects under our eye, some of which seemed to obstruct the view of others equally interesting;—the Valley of Ice, the Needles, Mont Blanc, with the snowy mountains below, finely contrasted with Breven, and the green hills on the opposite side of Chamouni, and the sun in full splendor showing all of them to the greatest advantage.—The whole forms a scene equally sublime and beautiful, far above my power of description, and worthy of the eloquence of that very ingenious gentleman, who has so finely illustrated these subjects, in a particular treatise, and given so many examples of both in his parliamentary speeches.

While we remained in contemplation of this scene, some of the company observed, that from the top of one of the Needles the prospect would be still more magnificent, as the eye could stretch over Breven, beyond Geneva, all the way to Mount Jura, and comprehend the Pays de Vallais, and many other mountains and vallies.

This excited the ambition of the D—— of H——. He sprung up, and made towards the Aiguille du Dru, which is the highest of the four Needles. Though he bounded over the ice with the elasticity of a young chamois, it was a considerable time before he could arrive at the foot of the Needle:— for people are greatly deceived as to distances, in those snowy regions.

Should he get near the top, said Mr. G——, looking after him with eagerness, he will swear we have seen nothing—But I will try to mount as high as he can;—I am not fond of seeing people above me. So saying, he sprung after him.

In a short time we saw them both scrambling up the rock:—The D—— had gained a considerable height, when he was suddenly stopped by a part of the rock which was perfectly impracticable (for his impetuosity had prevented him from choosing the easiest way); so Mr. G—— overtook him.

Here they had time to breathe and cool a little. The one being determined not to be surpassed, the other thought the exploit not worth his while, since the honour must be divided. So like two rival powers, who have exhausted their strength by a fruitless contest, they returned, fatigued and disappointed, to the place from which they had set out.

After a very agreeable repast, on the provisions and wine which our guides had brought from the Prieuré, we passed, by an easy descent, from the green part of Montanvert to the Valley of Ice. A walk upon this frozen sea is attended with inconveniencies. In some places, the swellings, which have been compared to waves, are forty or fifty feet high: yet, as they are rough, and the ice intermingled with snow, one may walk over them. In other parts, those waves are of a very moderate size, and in some places the surface is quite level.

What renders a passage over this valley still more difficult and dangerous is, the rents in the ice, which are to be met with, whatever direction you follow. These rents are from two to six feet wide, and of an amazing depth; reaching from the surface of the valley, through a body of ice many hundred fathoms thick. On throwing down a stone, or any other solid substance, we could hear the hollow murmur of its descent for a very long time, sounding like far distant waves breaking upon rocks.

Our guides, emboldened by habit, skipped over these rents without any sign of fear, though they informed us, that they had often seen fresh clefts formed, while they walked on the valley. They added, indeed, for our encouragement, that this was always preceded by a loud continued noise, which gave warning of what was to happen.

It is evident, however, that this warning, though it should always precede the rent, could be of little use to those who had advanced to the middle of the valley; for they neither could know certainly in what direction to run, nor could they have time to get off: and in case the ice should yawn directly under their feet, they must inevitably perish.—But probably few accidents of that kind happen; and this has greater influence, than any reasoning upon the subject.

It is supposed, that the snow and ice at the bottom melting by the warmth of the earth, leave great vacancies, in the form of vaults. These natural arches support for a long time an amazing weight of ice and snow;—for there is a vast distance from the bottom to the surface of this valley.—But the ice beneath continuing to dissolve, and the snow above to increase, the arches must at last give way, which occasions the noise and rents above mentioned. Water, also, which may have fallen from the surface into the clefts, or is lodged by any means in this great mass of snow, will, by its sudden expansion in the act of freezing, occasion new rents at the surface.

We had heard a great deal of the havoc made by avalanches. These are formed of snow driven by the winds against the highest and most protuberant parts of rocks and mountains, where it hardens and adheres sometimes till a prodigious mass is accumulated. But when these supporters are able to sustain the increasing weight no longer, the avalanche falls at once, hurrying large portions of the loosened rock or mountain along with it;—and rolling from a vast height, with a thundering noise, to the valley, involves in certain destruction all the trees, houses, cattle, and men, which lie in its way[2].

The greater part of those who have made a journey to the Glaciers have seen one or more of these avalanches in the very act of falling, and have themselves always escaped by miracle.—Just as most people who have made a single voyage by sea, if it were only between Dover and Calais, have met with a storm, and very narrowly escaped shipwreck.

All that any of our party can boast is, that during the nights we lay at Chamouni, we frequently heard a noise like distant thunder, which we were told was occasioned by the falling of some of these same avalanches at a few miles distance. And during our excursions, we saw trees destroyed, and tracts of soil torn from the sides of the mountains, over which the avalanches were said to have rolled, two or three years before we passed. These were the narrowest escapes we made.—I heartily wish the same good luck to all travellers, whatever account they themselves may choose to give to their friends, when they return.

The Valley of Ice is several leagues in length, and not above a quarter of a league in breadth. It divides into branches, which run behind the chain of mountains formerly taken notice of. It appears like a frozen amphitheatre, and is bounded by mountains, in whose clefts columns of crystal, as we were informed, are to be found.—The hoary majesty of Mont Blanc … I was in danger of rising into poetry, when recollecting the story of Icarus, I thought it best not to trust to my own waxen wings.—I beg leave rather to borrow the following lines, which will please you better than any flight of mine, and prevent me from a fall:

> So Zembla's rocks (the beauteous work of frost)
>
> Rise white in air, and glitter o'er the coast,
>
> Pale suns, unfelt, at distance roll away,
>
> And on th' impassive ice the lightnings play;
>
> Eternal snows the growing mass supply,
>
> Fill the bright mountains, prop th' incumbent sky;
>
> As Atlas fix'd, each hoary pile appears,

The gather'd winter of a thousand years.

Having walked a considerable time on the valley, and being sufficiently regaled with ice, we at length thought of returning to our cottage at Prieuré. Our guides led us down by a shorter and deeper way than that by which we had ascended; and in about two hours after we had begun our descent, we found ourselves at the bottom of the mountain. This rapid manner of descending, most people find more severe upon the muscles of the legs and thighs, than even the ascent. For my own part, I was very near exhausted; and as we were still a couple of miles distant from our lodgings, it was with the greatest satisfaction that I saw our obsequious mules in waiting to carry us to our cottage; where having at last arrived, and being assembled in a small room, excluded from the view of icy valleys, crystal hills, and snowy mountains, with nothing before us but humble objects, as cold meat, coarse bread, and poor wine, we contrived to pass an hour before going to bed, in talking over the exploits of the day, and the wonders we had seen.—Whether there is greater pleasure in this, or in viewing the scenes themselves, is a question not yet decided by the casuists.

[2]

Ac veluti montis Saxum de vertice præceps

Cum ruit avulsum vento, seu turbidus imber

Proluit, aut annis solvit sublapsa vetustas:

Fertur in abruptum magno mons improbus actu,

Exultatque solo, silvas, armenta, virosque

Involvens secum.

VIRG.

LETTER XXVI.

Geneva.

There are five or six different Glaciers, which all terminate upon one side of the Valley of Chamouni, within the space of about five leagues.

These are prodigious collections of snow and ice, formed in the intervals or hollows, between the mountains that bound the side of the valley near which Mount Blanc stands.

The snow in those hollows being screened from the influence of the sun, the heat of summer can dissolve only a certain portion of it. These magazines of ice and snow are not formed by what falls directly from the heavens into the intervals. They are supplied by the snow which falls during winter on the loftiest parts of Mont Blanc; large beds or strata of which slide down imperceptibly by their own gravity, and finding no resistance at these intervals, they form long irregular roots around all the adjacent mountains.

Five of these enter, by five different embouchures, into the valley of Chamouni, and are called Glaciers, on one of which we had been.

At present their surface is from a thousand, or two thousand feet high, above the valley.

Their breadth depends on the wideness of the interval between the mountains in which they are formed.

Viewed from the valley, they have, in my opinion, a much finer effect than from their summit.

The rays of the sun striking with various force on the different parts, according as they are more or less exposed, occasion an unequal dissolution of the ice; and, with the help of a little imagination, give the appearances of columns, arches, and turrets, which are in some places transparent.

A fabric of ice in this taste, two thousand feet high, and three times as broad, with the sun shining full upon it, you must acknowledge to be a very singular piece of architecture.

Our company ascended only the Glacier of Montanvert, which is not the highest, and were contented with a view of the others from the valley; but more curious travellers will surely think it worth their labour, to examine each of them more particularly.

Some people are so fond of Glaciers, that not satisfied with their present size, they insist positively, that they must necessarily grow larger every year, and they argue the matter thus:

The present existence of the Glaciers is a sufficient proof that there has, at some period or other, been a greater quantity of snow formed during the winter, than the heat of the summer has been able to dissolve. But this disproportion must necessarily increase every year, and, of consequence, the Glaciers must augment: because, any given quantity of snow and ice remaining through the course of one summer, must increase the cold of the atmosphere around it in some degree; which being reinforced by the snows of the succeeding winter, will refill: the dissolving power of the sun more the second summer than the first, and still more the third than the second, and so on.

The conclusion of this reasoning is, that the Glaciers must grow larger by an increasing ratio every year, till the end of time. For this reason, the authors of this theory regret, that they themselves have been sent into the world so soon; because, if their birth had been delayed for nine or ten thousand years, they should have seen the Glaciers in much greater glory, Mont Blanc being but a Lilliputian at present, in comparison of what it will be then.

However rational this may appear, objections have nevertheless been suggested, which I am sorry for; because, when a theory is tolerably consistent, well fabricated, and goodly to behold, nothing can be more vexatious, than to see a plodding officious fellow overthrow the whole structure at once, by a dash of his pen, as Harlequin does a house with a touch of his sword, in a pantomime entertainment.

Such cavillers say, that as the Glaciers augment in size, there must be a greater extent of surface for the sun-beams to act upon, and, of consequence, the dissolution will be greater, which must effectually prevent the continual increase contended for.

But the other party extricate themselves from this difficulty by roundly asserting, that the additional cold occasioned by the snow and ice already deposited, has a much greater influence in retarding their dissolution, than the increased surface can have in hastening it: and in confirmation of their system, they tell you, that the oldest inhabitants of Chamouni remember the Glaciers when they were much smaller than at present; and also remember the time when they could walk, from the Valley of Ice, to places behind the mountains, by passages which are now quite choked up with hills of snow, not above fifty years old.

Whether the inhabitants of Chamouni assert this from a laudable partiality to the Glaciers, whom they may now consider (on account of their drawing strangers to visit the Valley) as their best neighbours;—or from politeness to the supporters of the above-mentioned opinion;—or from real observation, I shall not presume to say.—But I myself have heard several of the old people in Chamouni assert the fact.

The cavillers being thus obliged to relinquish their former objection, attempt, in the next place, to show, that the above theory leads to an absurdity; because, say they, If the Glaciers go on increasing in bulk ad infinitum, the globe itself would become in process of time a mere appendage to Mont Blanc.

The advocates for the continual augmentation of the Glaciers reply, that as this inconveniency has not already happened, there needs no other refutation of the impious doctrine of certain philosophers, who assert that the world has existed from eternity; and as to the globe's becoming an appendage to the mountain, they assure us, that the world will be at an end long before that event can happen. So that those of the most timid natures, and most delicate constitutions, may dismiss their fears on that subject.

For my own part, though I wish well to the Glaciers, and all the inhabitants of Chamouni, having passed some days very pleasantly in their company; I will take no part in this controversy, the merits of which I leave to your own judgment.

LETTER XXVII.

Geneva.

The morning of the day on which we departed from Prieuré, I observed a girl of a very singular appearance sitting before the door of one of the houses. When I spoke to her, she made no answer: But an elderly man, who had been a soldier in the king of Sardinia's service, and my acquaintance since the moment of our arrival, informed me, that this girl was an idiot, and had been so from her birth.

He took me to two other houses in the village, in each of which there was one person in the same melancholy situation; and he assured me, that all over the valley of Chamouni, in a family consisting of five or six children, one of them, generally speaking, was a perfect natural.

This was confirmed by some others, to whom I afterwards mentioned it. I was told at the same time, that the parents, so far from considering this as a misfortune, looked upon it as an indication of good luck to the rest of the family, and no unhappiness to the individual, whom they always cherish and protect with the utmost tenderness.

I asked my soldier, if any of his own family were in that situation? Non, Monsieur, answered he; et aussi j'ai passé une vie bien dure.

Don't you think these poor creatures very unhappy?

Demande pardon, Monsieur:—Ils sont très heureux—

But you would not like to have been born in that state yourself?

Vous croyez donc, Monsieur, que j'aurois été bien attrapé?

Attrapé!—certainly:—don't you think so too?

Pour cela, non, Monsieur; je n'aurois jamais travaillé.—

To one who has through life been obliged to work hard for a bare subsistence, labour appears the greatest evil, and perfect idleness the greatest blessing. If this soldier had been brought up in idleness, and had experienced all the horrors and dejection which attend indolent luxury, very possibly he would be of a different opinion.

During this journey, I remarked, that in some particular villages, and for a considerable tract of country, scarcely was there any body to be seen who had that swelling of the throat and neck, which is thought so general among all the inhabitants of the Alps. In particular, I did not observe any body at Prieuré with this complaint; and, upon enquiry, was informed, that there are many parishes in which not a single person is troubled with it, and that in other places at no great distance it is almost universal.

In the valley of Chamouni there is only one hamlet where it is common; but in the Pays de Vallais, I was told, it is more frequent than in any other place.

As this disease seems to be endemical, it cannot, as has been imagined, proceed from the drinking of water impregnated with snow or ice; for this beverage is common to all the inhabitants of the Alps, and of other mountains.

If the water be in reality the vehicle of this disease, we must suppose it impregnated not only with dissolved ice and snow, but also with some salt, or other substance, possessed of the noxious quality of obstructing the glands of the throat; and we must also suppose, that this noxious substance is to be found in no other inhabited place but the Alps.

After one of the inhabitants of Chamouni had enumerated many parishes where there were, and others where there were no Goîtres (which is the name they give this swelling), he concluded by telling me, I should see them in great abundance among the Valaisans, to whose country we were going.—When I told the man, I thought his country-people very happy, in being quite free from such an odious disease, which afflicted their poor neighbours—En revanche, said the peasant, nous sommes accablés des impôts;—et dans le pays de Vallais on ne paye rien.

The d——l is in the fellow, exclaimed I.—Were it in your choice, would you accept of Goîtres, to get free of taxes?

Très volontiers, Monsieur;—l'un vaut bien l'autre.

> Quid causæ est, merito quin illis Jupiter ambas,
>
> Iratas buccas inflet.

You see, my friend, that it is not in courts and capitals alone that men are discontented with their fortunes. The causes of repining are different in different places; but the effect is the same every where.

On the morning of the sixth day, we bid adieu to Prieuré; and having ascended the mountains, which shut up the valley of Chamouni at the end opposite to that by which we had entered, after various windings on a very rugged road, we gradually descended into a hollow of the most dismal appearance.

It is surrounded with high, bare, rugged rocks, without trees or verdure of any kind, the bottom being as barren and craggy as the sides, and the whole forming a most hideous landscape. This dreary valley is of a considerable length, but very narrow. I imagine it would have pleased the fancy of Salvator, who might have been tempted to steal a corner of it for one of his pieces, which, when he had enlivened with a murder or two, would have been a master-piece of the Horrible.

Having traversed this, we continued our journey, sometimes ascending, then descending into other vallies whose names I have forgot.—We had a long continued ascent over Mount Noir, a very high hill, covered with pine-trees, many of which are above a hundred feet in height. I was obliged to walk on foot most of this road, which is full as steep as any part of that by which we had ascended Montanvert.

We came at length to the pass which separates the King of Sardinia's country from the little republic, called the Pays de Vallais. Across this there is an old thick wall, and a gate, without any guard. This narrow pass continues for several miles.—A few peasants arranged along the upper part of the mountains could, by rolling down stones, destroy a whole army, if it should attempt to enter into the country by this road.

When you have patted through this long defile, the road runs along the side of a high and steep mountain; but is still so very narrow, that two persons cannot with safety go abreast, and all passengers are entirely at the mercy of those who may be posted on the higher parts of the mountain.

From the side of the mountain on which we passed, we could have spoken to the people who inhabited the side of the mountain opposite. But I am convinced it would have taken three or four hours walking, to have gone to them: Because we must, by a long, oblique tour, have first reached the bottom of the cleft between us, and then have ascended to them, by another long, fatiguing path, which could not be done in less time than I have mentioned.

Wherever there is a spot of the mountain tolerably fertile, and the slope less formidable than usual, you are almost certain to find a peasant's house. All the houses are built of the fine red pine, which grows near at hand. The carriage of this, even for a short way, upon those very steep mountains, must have been attended with no small difficulty and danger. These dwellings are raised on wooden props, or pillars, two or three feet above the ground. On the top of each pillar a large flag or broad stone is placed, to obstruct the entrance of rats.—Indeed the situation of these abodes is so very aerial, that they seem almost inaccessible to every animal that has not wings, as well as to rats.

The road led us at length to the summit, which is level, and covered with pines for several miles. Having traversed this, and descended a little on the other side, the lower Vallais opened to our view. Nothing can be imagined more singularly picturesque:—It is of an oval form, about seven leagues in length, and one in breadth, surrounded on all sides by mountains of a stupendous height, the lower parts of which are covered with very rich pasture.—The valley itself is fertile in the highest degree, finely cultivated, and divided into meadows, gardens, and vineyards. The Rhone flows in beautiful mazes from the one end to the other.—Sion, the capital of the Vallais, is situated on the upper extremity, and the town of Martigny on the lower, many villages and detached houses appearing all over the valley between them. The prospect we had now under our eye formed a striking and agreeable contrast with the scenes we had just left. The distance from this point to Martigny, which stands near the bottom of the mountain, is about six miles. There is one continued descent the whole way, which is rendered easy by the roads being thrown into a zig-zag direction.

After the rugged paths we had been accustomed to, it was, comparatively speaking, rest, to walk down this mountain.—We arrived at Martigny refreshed, and in high spirits.

LETTER XXVIII.

Geneva.

During our journey over the mountains which encircle the lower Vallais, I had often felt an inclination to enter some of the peasants' houses, that I might be a witness of the domestic œconomy of a people which Rousseau has so delightfully described.

Had I been alone, or with a single companion, I should have pledged them liberally, and made a temporary sacrifice of my reason to the Penates of those happy mountaineers; for, according to him, this is the only payment they will receive for their entertainment: But our company was by far too numerous, and would have put their hospitality to too severe a trial.

After a night's refreshment at Martigny, we looked with some degree of impatience for the cabriolets, which had been ordered to meet us there. We all talked with rapture of the sublime scenes from which we had descended; yet nobody regretted that the rest of the journey was to be performed on plain ground. The cabriolets arriving the same forenoon, we set out by the *embouchure*, which leads to St. Maurice.

That immense rampart of mountains which surrounds the Vallais at every other part, is cut through here, which renders that country accessible to the inhabitants of the canton of Bern. This opening has the appearance of a vast and magnificent avenue, on each side of which a row of lofty mountains are placed, instead of trees. It is some leagues in length. The ground is exceedingly fertile, and perfectly level: Yet if an attack were suspected, this pass could be easily defended by batteries at the bottom of the mountains on each side. Besides, a river of considerable depth flows along, sometimes on the one side, and sometimes on the other, and, by continually crossing the plain, seems to forbid all hostile incroachments.

This little spot, the country of the Vallaisans, which comprehends the valley above described, the mountains that surround it, and stretch on one side all the way to the lake, including three or four towns and many villages, is a district, governed by its own laws and magistrates, in alliance with, but independent of, the Swiss cantons, or any other power. The religion is popery, and the form of government democratic.—It seems to have been imagined by Nature as a last asylum for that divinity, without whose influence all her other gifts are of small value. Should the rapacious hand of despotism ever crush the rights of mankind, and overturn the altars of FREEDOM, in every other country in Europe, a chosen people may here preserve the true worship, and share her regard with the provinces beyond the Atlantic.

In the middle of the opening above mentioned, about four leagues from Martigny, between two high mountains, and at the side of the Rhone, is situated the little town of St. Maurice, which guards this entrance into the lower Vallais.

Having passed a bridge at this town, which divides the country of the Vallaisans from the canton of Bern, we proceeded to Bex, a village remarkable for its delightful situation, and for the salt-works which are near it. After dinner, we visited these. We entered the largest saline by a passage cut out of the solid rock, of a sufficient height and breadth to allow a man to walk with ease.

Travellers who have the curiosity to explore these gloomy abodes, are previously furnished with lighted lamps or torches, and dressed in a coarse habit, to defend them from the slimy drippings which fall from the roof and sides of the passage.

Upon arriving at the reservoir of salt water, which is about three quarters of a mile from the entrance, I was seized with a nausea, from the disagreeable smell of the place, and returned with all possible expedition to the open air, leaving my companions to push their researches as far as they pleased. They remained a considerable time after me. What satisfaction they received within, I shall not take upon me to determine; but I never saw a set of people make a more melancholy exit;—with their greasy frocks, their torches, their smoky, woe-begone countenances, they put me in mind of a procession of condemned heretics, walking to the flames, at an Auto de Fè at Lisbon.

Having recovered their looks and spirits at the inn at Bex, they allured me, that the curiosities they had seen during their subterraneous progress, particularly after my secession, were more worthy of observation than any thing we had met with since we had left Geneva; and they all advised me, with affected seriousness, to return and complete the interesting visit which I had left unfinished.

Next morning our company divided, the D—— of H—— and Mr. G—— chusing to return by Vevay and Lausanne. Mr U——, Mr. K——, and myself, went by the other side of the lake of Geneva. They took with them the two chaises, and we proceeded on horseback, our road not admitting of wheel-carriages.

We left Bex early in the morning, passing through Aigle, a thriving little town, whose houses are built of a white marble found in the neighbourhood.—The ideas of gloom and wretchedness, as well as of magnificence, had somehow been linked in my mind with this substance.—I don't know whether this is owing to its being used in tombs and monuments;—or to my having observed, that the houses most profusely ornamented by it are so often the mansions of dulness and discontent.—Whatever gave rise to this connection of ideas, the appearance of the inhabitants of Aigle was well calculated to cure me of the prejudice; for although the meanest houses in this poor little town are built of marble, yet in the course of my life I never beheld less care and more satisfaction in the countenances of any set of people. An appearance of ease and content prevails not only here, but all over Switzerland.

A little beyond Aigle, we crossed the Rhone in boats. It is broader at this ferry, than where it flows from the lake of Geneva. As soon as we arrived on the other side, we were again in the dominions of the Vallaisans, which extend on this side all the way to the lake.

We had a delightful ride to St. Gingo, where we dined, and remained several hours to refresh our horses. Though it was Sunday, there was a fair at this town, to which such a concourse of people had resorted from the Pays de Vallais, the canton of Bern, and from Savoy, that we could not without difficulty find a room to dine in.

The dress of the young Vallaisannes is remarkably picturesque. A little silk hat, fixed on one side of the head, from which a bunch of ribbons hangs negligently, with a jacket very advantageous to the shape, gives them a smart air, and is upon the whole more becoming than the dress of the common people in any country I have yet seen.

A little beyond St. Gingo, we entered the dukedom of Savoy. The road is here cut out of the lofty rocks which rise from the lake of Geneva. It must be passed with caution, being exceedingly narrow, and no fence to prevent the traveller from falling over a very high precipice into the lake, in case his horse should start to one side.

At some places this narrow road is rendered still more dangerous by fragments which have fallen from the mountains above, and have impaired and almost destroyed the path. At those places we were obliged to dismount, and lead our horses, with great attention, over rubbish and broken rocks, till we gained those parts of the road which were intire.

The sight of Meillerie brought to my remembrance the charming letters of Rousseau's two lovers. This recollection filled me with a pleasing enthusiasm. I sought with my eyes, and imagined I discovered the identical place where St. Preux sat with his telescope to view the habitation of his beloved Julia.— I traced in my imagination his route, when he sprung from rock to rock after one of her letters, which a sudden gust of wind had snatched from his hands.—I marked the point at which the two lovers embarked to return to Clarence, after an evening visit to those very rocks,—when St. Preux, agonized with tender recollections, and distracted with despair, was tempted to seize his mistress, then the wife of another, and precipitate himself along with her, from the boat headlong into the middle of the lake.

Every circumstance of that pathetic story came fresh into my mind. I felt myself on a kind of classic ground, and experienced that the eloquence of that inimitable writer had given me an interest in the landscape before my eyes, beyond that which its own natural beauties could have effected.

Having left the romantic rocks of Meillerie behind, we descended to a fertile plain, almost on a level with the lake, along which the road runs, flanked with rows of fine tall trees all the way to Evian, an agreeable little town, renowned for its mineral waters. Here we met with many of our Geneva acquaintances of both sexes, who had come, under pretence of drinking the waters, to amuse themselves in this delightful retreat.

We next proceeded to Tonon, a most religious city, if we may judge by the number of churches and monasteries which it contains. The number of inhabitants are calculated at six or seven thousand, and every seventh person I saw wore the uniform of some religious order. After this, I was not greatly surprised to perceive every symptom of poverty among the lay inhabitants.

Having bespoke supper and beds at this place, we went and visited the convent of Carthusians at Ripaille, which is at a little distance.

It was here that a Duke of Savoy, after a fortunate reign, assumed the character of a hermit, and lived with the fathers a life of piety and mortification, according to some; of voluptuousness and policy, according to others. What we are well assured of is, that he was in a short time elected Pope, by the council of Basil, which dignity he was obliged to relinquish nine years after, having first made very honourable conditions for himself. After this, he spent the remainder of his life with the reputation of great sanctity at Ripaille.

Had he been allowed to chuse any part of Europe for his retreat, he could not have found one more agreeable than this which his own dominions furnished.

The fathers with great politeness showed us their forest, their gardens, their apartments, and a very elegant new chapel, which is just finished. They then conducted us into the chamber where their Sovereign had lived and died. They talked much of his genius, his benevolence, and his sanctity. We heard them with every mark of acquiescence, and returned to our inn, where tho' *we* certainly did not *faire Ripaille*, I'm convinced the fleas did: As Shakespeare's carrier says, there was never a King in Christendom better bit than we were, through the whole night. We paid for our entertainment, such as it was, a very extravagant bill in the morning, and without grudging; for we considered, that we were to leave our host and his family amongst a swarm of blood-suckers, still more intolerable than fleas.

We arrived the same forenoon at Geneva, having finished a tour in which a greater variety of sublime and interesting objects offer themselves to the contemplation of the traveller, than can be found in any other part of the globe of the same extent.

I am &c.

LETTER XXIX.

Geneva.

I am not surprised that your inquiries of late entirely regard the philosopher of Ferney. This extraordinary person has contrived to excite more curiosity, and to retain the attention of Europe for a longer space of time, than any other man this age has produced, monarchs and heroes included.—Even the most trivial anecdote relating to him seems, in some degree, to interest the Public.

Since I have been in this country, I have had frequent opportunities of conversing with him, and still more with those who have lived in intimacy with him for many years; so that, whatever remarks I may send you on this subject, are founded either on my own observation, or on that of the most candid and intelligent of his acquaintance.

He has enemies and admirers here, as he has every where else; and not unfrequently both united in the same person.

The first idea which has presented itself to all who have attempted a description of his person, is that of a skeleton. In as far as this implies excessive leanness, it is just; but it must be remembered, that this skeleton, this mere composition of skin and bone, has a look of more spirit and vivacity, than is generally produced by flesh and blood, however blooming and youthful.

The most piercing eyes I ever beheld are those of Voltaire, now in his eightieth year. His whole countenance is expressive of genius, observation, and extreme sensibility.

In the morning he has a look of anxiety and discontent; but this gradually wears off, and after dinner he seems cheerful:—yet an air of irony never entirely forsakes his face, but may always be observed lurking in his features, whether he frowns or smiles.

When the weather is favourable, he takes an airing in his coach, with his niece, or with some of his guests, of whom there is always a sufficient number at Ferney. Sometimes he saunters in his garden; or if the weather does not permit him to go abroad, he employs his leisure-hours in playing at chess with Pere Adam; or in receiving the visits of strangers, a continual succession of whom attend at Ferney to catch an opportunity of seeing him; or in dictating and reading letters; for he still retains correspondents in all the countries of Europe, who inform him of every remarkable occurrence, and send him every new literary production as soon as it appears.

By far the greater part of his time is spent in his study; and whether he reads himself, or listens to another, he always has a pen in his hand, to take notes, or make remarks.

Composition is his principal amusement. No author who writes for daily bread, no young poet ardent for distinction, is more assiduous with his pen, or more anxious for fresh fame, than the wealthy and applauded Seigneur of Ferney.

He lives in a very hospitable manner, and takes care always to keep a good cook. He has generally two or three visitors from Paris, who stay with him a month or six weeks at a time. When they go, their places are soon supplied; so that there is a constant rotation of society at Ferney. These, with Voltaire's own family, and his visitors from Geneva, compose a company of twelve or fourteen people, who dine daily at his table, whether he appears or not. For when engaged preparing some new production for the press, indisposed or in bad spirits, he does not dine with the company; but satisfies himself with seeing them for a few minutes, either before or after dinner.

All who bring recommendations from his friends, may depend upon being received, if he be not really indisposed.—He often presents himself to the strangers, who assemble almost every afternoon in his anti-chamber, although they bring no particular recommendation. But sometimes they are obliged to retire without having their curiosity gratified.

As often as this happens, he is sure of being accused of peevishness; and a thousand ill-natured stories are related, perhaps invented, out of revenge, because he is not in the humour of being exhibited like a dancing bear on a holiday. It is much less surprising that he sometimes refuses, than that he should comply so often. In him, this complaisance must proceed solely from a desire to oblige; for Voltaire has been so long accustomed to admiration, that the stare of a few strangers cannot be supposed to afford him much pleasure.

His niece, Madame Denis, does the honours of the table, and entertains the company, when her uncle is not able, or does not choose to appear. She is a well-disposed woman, who behaves with good-humour to every body, and with unremitting attention and tenderness to her uncle.

The forenoon is not a proper time to visit Voltaire. He cannot bear to have his hours of study interrupted. This alone is sufficient to put him out of humour; besides, he is then apt to be querulous, whether he suffers by the infirmities of age or from some accidental cause of chagrin. Whatever is the reason, he is less an optimist at that part of the day than at any other.—It was in the morning, probably, that he remarked,—que c'étoit dommage que le quinquina se trouvoit en Amérique, et la fièvre en nos climats.

Those who are invited to supper, have an opportunity of seeing him in the most advantageous point of view. He then exerts himself to entertain the company, and seems as fond of saying, what are called good things, as ever:—and when any lively remark or bon mot comes from another, he is equally delighted, and pays the fullest tribute of applause.—The spirit of mirth gains upon him by indulgence.—When surrounded by his friends, and animated by the presence of women, he seems to enjoy life with all the sensibility of youth. His genius then surmounts the restraints of age and infirmity, and flows along in a fine strain of pleasing, spirited observation, and delicate irony.

He has an excellent talent of adapting his conversation to his company.— The first time the D—— of H—— waited on him, he turned the discourse on the ancient alliance between the French and Scotch nations.—Reciting the circumstance of one of his Grace's predecessors having accompanied Mary Queen of Scots, whose heir he at that time was, to the court of France,—he spoke of the heroic characters of his ancestors, the ancient Earls of Douglas—of the great literary reputation of some of his countrymen, then living; and mentioned the names of Hume and Robertson in terms of high approbation.

A short time afterwards, he was visited by two Russian Noblemen, who are now at Geneva. Voltaire talked to them a great deal of their Empress, and the flourishing state of their country.—Formerly, said he, your countrymen were guided by ignorant priests,—the arts were unknown, and your lands lay waste;—but now the arts flourish, and the lands are cultivated.—One of the young men replied, That there was still a great proportion of barren land in Russia.—At least, said Voltaire, you must admit, that of late your country has been very *fertile in laurels*.

His dislike to the clergy is well known.—This leads him to join in a very trite topic of abuse with people who have no pretension to that degree of wit which alone could make their railings tolerable.—The conversation happening to turn into this channel, one person said, If you substract pride from priests, nothing will remain.—Vous comptez donc, Monsieur, la gourmandise, pour rien, said Voltaire.

He approves much more of Marmontel's Art of Poetry, than of any poems of that author's composition. Speaking of these, he said that Marmontel, like Moses, could guide others to the Holy Land, though he was not allowed to enter it himself[3].

Voltaire's unbecoming allusions to the Sacred Writings, and his attempts to turn into ridicule some of the most venerable characters mentioned in them, are notorious.

A certain person, who stammered very much, found means to get himself introduced at Ferney.—He had no other recommendation than the praises he very liberally bestowed on himself.—When he left the room Voltaire said, he supposed him to be an avanturier, un imposteur.—Madame Denis said, Impostors never stammer:—To which Voltaire replied—Moïse, ne begayoit-il pas?

You must have heard of the animosity which has long subsisted between Voltaire and Freron the Journalist at Paris. The former was walking one day in his garden with a gentleman from Geneva. A toad crawled across the road before them:—The gentleman, to please Voltaire, said, pointing at the toad,—There is a Freron.—What can that poor animal have done to you, replied the Wit, to deserve such a name?

He compared the British nation to a hogshead of their own strong beer; the top of which is froth, the bottom dregs, the middle excellent.

A friend of Voltaire's having recommended to his perusal, a particular system of metaphysics, supported by a train of reasonings, by which the author displayed his own ingenuity and address, without convincing the mind of the reader, or proving any thing besides his own eloquence and sophistry, asked, some time after, the critic's opinion of this performance?

Metaphysical writers, replied Voltaire, are like minuet-dancers; who being dressed to the greatest advantage, make a couple of bows, move through the room in the finest attitudes, display all their graces, are in continual motion without advancing a step, and finish at the identical point from which they set out. Perhaps he borrowed this thought from the following lines in Pope's Dunciad:

> Or set on metaphysic ground to prance,
>
> Show all his paces, not a step advance.

This, I hope, will satisfy you for the present; in my next, I shall send you what farther particulars I think worth your notice concerning this singular man.—Mean while, I am, &c.

---

[3] The same allusion, though probably Voltaire did not know it, was long since made by Cowley—

Bacon like Moses led us forth at last

> The barren wilderness he past,
>
> Did on the very border stand
>
> Of the blest promised land,
>
> And from the mountain top of his exalted wit
>
> Saw it himself, and shewed us it.

LETTER XXX.

Geneva.

Considered as a matter, Voltaire appears in a very amiable light. He is affable, humane, and generous to his tenants and dependants. He loves to see them prosper; and takes part in their private and domestic concerns, with the attention of a patriarch.—He promotes industry and manufactures among them, by every means he can devise: by his care and patronage alone, Ferney, from a wretched village, whose inhabitants were sunk in sloth and poverty, is become a flourishing and commodious little town.

That acrimony, which appears in some of Voltaire's works, seems to be excited only against rival wits, and contemporary writers, who refuse him that distinguished place on Parnassus, to which his talents entitle him.

If he has been the author of severe satire, he has also been the object of a great deal. Who has been the aggressor, it would be difficult to determine; but it must be confessed, that where he has not been irritated as a writer, he appears a good-humoured man; and, in particular instances, displays a true philanthropy.—The whole of his conduct respecting the Calas family;—his protection of the Sirvens, his patronage of the young lady descended from Corneille, and many examples, which might be mentioned, are all of this nature.

Some people will tell you, that all the bustle he made, on these, and similar occasions, proceeded from vanity; but in my mind, the man who takes pains to justify oppressed innocence, to rouse the indignation of mankind against cruelty, and to relieve indigent merit, is in reality benevolent, however vain he may be of such actions.—Such a man is unquestionably a more useful member of society, than the humblest monk, who has no other plan in life, than the working out his own salvation in a corner.

Voltaire's criticisms on the writings of Shakespear do him no honour; they betray an ignorance of the author, whose works he so rashly condemns. Shakespear's irregularities, and his disregard for the unities of the drama, are obvious to the dullest of modern critics; but Voltaire's national prejudices, and his imperfect knowledge of the language, render him blind to some of the most shining beauties of the English Poet; his remarks, however, though not always candid nor delicate, are for the most part lively.

One evening, at Ferney, the conversation happening to turn on the genius of Shakespear, Voltaire expatiated on the impropriety and absurdity of introducing low characters and vulgar dialogue into Tragedy; and gave many instances of the English bard's having offended in that particular, even in his most pathetic plays. A gentleman of the company, who is a great admirer of Shakespear, observed, by way of palliation, that though those characters were low, yet they were natural (dans la nature, was his expression). Avec permission, Monsieur, replied Voltaire, mon cul est bien dans la nature, et cependant je porte des coulottes.

Voltaire had formerly a little theatre at his own house, where dramatic pieces were represented by some of the society who visited there, he himself generally taking some important character; but by all accounts this was not his fort, nature having fitted him for conceiving the sentiments, but not representing the actions of a hero.

Mr. Cramer of Geneva sometimes assisted upon these occasions.—I have often seen that gentleman act at a private theatre in that city with deserved applause. Very few of those who have made acting the study and business of their lives, could have represented the characters in which he appeared, with more judgment and energy.

The celebrated Clairon herself has been proud to tread Voltaire's domestic theatre, and to display at once his genius and her own.

These dramatic entertainments at Ferney, to which many of the inhabitants of Geneva were, from time to time, invited, in all probability increased their desire for such amusements, and gave the hint to a company of French comedians, to come every summer to the neighbourhood.

As the Syndics and Council did not judge it proper to license their acting, this company have erected a theatre at Chatelaine, which is on the French side of the ideal line which separates that kingdom from the territories of the Republic, and about three miles from the ramparts of Geneva.

People come occasionally from Savoy and Switzerland to attend these representations; but the company on which the actors chiefly depend, are the citizens of Geneva. The play begins at three or four in the afternoon, that the spectators may have time to return before the shutting of the gates.

I have been frequently at this theatre. The performers are moderately good. The admired Le Kain, who is now at Ferney, on a visit to Voltaire, sometimes exhibits:—but when I go, my chief inducement is to see Voltaire, who generally attends when Le Kain acts, and when one of his own tragedies is to be represented.

He sits on the stage, and behind the scenes; but so as to be seen by a great part of the audience. He takes as much interest in the representation, as if his own character depended on the performance. He seems perfectly chagrined and disgusted when any of the actors commit a mistake; and when he thinks they perform well, never fails to mark his approbation with all the violence of voice and gesture.

He enters into the feigned distresses of the piece with every symptom of real emotion, and even sheds tears with the profusion of a girl present for the first time at a tragedy.

I have sometimes sat near him during the whole entertainment, observing with astonishment such a degree of sensibility in a man of eighty. This great age, one would naturally believe, might have considerably blunted every sensation, particularly those occasioned by the fictitious distresses of the drama, to which he has been habituated from his youth.

The pieces represented having been written by himself, is another circumstance which, in my opinion, should naturally tend to prevent their effect on him. Some people indeed assert that this, so far from diminishing, is the real cause of all his sensibility; and they urge, as a proof of this assertion that he attends the theatre only when some of his own pieces are to be acted.

That he should be better pleased to see his own tragedies represented than any others, is natural; but I do not readily comprehend, how he can be more easily moved and deceived, by distresses which he himself invented. Yet this degree of deception seems necessary to make a man shed tears. While these tears are flowing, he must believe the woes he weeps are real: he must have been so far deceived by the cunning of the scene, as to have forgot that he was in a playhouse. The moment he recollects that the whole is fiction, his sympathy and tears must cease.

I should be glad, however, to see Voltaire present at the representation of some of Corneille or Racine's tragedies, that I might observe whether he would discover more or less sensibility than he has done at his own. We should then be able to ascertain this curious, disputed point, whether his sympathy regarded the piece or the author.

Happy, if this extraordinary man had confined his genius to its native home, to the walks which the muses love, and where he has always been received with distinguished honour, and that he had never deviated from these, into the thorny paths of controversy! For while he attacked the tyrants and oppressors of mankind, and those who have perverted the benevolent nature of Christianity to the most selfish and malignant purposes, it is for ever to be regretted, that he allowed the shafts of his ridicule to glance upon the Christian religion itself.

By persevering in this, he has not only shocked the pious, but even disgusted infidels, who accuse him of borrowing from himself, and repeating the same argument in various publications; and seem as tired of the stale sneer against the Christian doctrines, as of the dullest and most tedious sermons in support of them.

Voltaire's behaviour during sickness has been represented in very opposite lights, I have heard much of his great contrition and repentance, when he had reason to believe his end approaching. These stories, had they been true, would have proved, that his infidelity was affectation, and that he was a believer and Christian in his heart.

I own I could never give any credit to such reports; for though I have frequently met with vain young men, who have given themselves airs of free-thinking, while in reality they were even superstitious, yet I never could understand what a man like Voltaire, or any man of common understanding, could propose to himself by such absurd affectation. To pretend to despise what we really revere, and to treat as human, what we believe to be divine, is certainly, of all kinds of hypocrisy, the most unpardonable.

I was at some pains to ascertain this matter; and I have been assured, by those who have lived during many years in familiarity with him, that all these stories are without foundation. They declared, that although he was unwilling to quit the enjoyment of life, and used the means of preserving health, he seemed no way afraid of the consequences of dying. That he never discovered, either in health or sickness, any remorse for the works imputed to him against the Christian religion.—That, on the contrary, he was blinded to such a degree, as to express uneasiness at the thoughts of dying before some of them, in which he was at that time engaged, were finished.

Though this conduct is not to be justified upon any supposition, yet there is more consistency, and, in my opinion, less wickedness in it, if we admit the account which his friends give, than there would be in his writing at once against the established opinions of mankind, the conviction of his own conscience, and the inspirations of the Deity, merely to acquire the applause of a few mistaken infidels.

However erroneous he may have been, I cannot suspect him of such absurdity. On the contrary, I imagine, that as soon as he is convinced of the truths of Christianity, he will openly avow his opinion, in health as in sickness, uniformly, to his last moment.

LETTER XXXI.

Geneva.

In obedience to your request, I shall give you my opinion freely with regard to Lord ———'s scheme of sending his two sons to be educated at Geneva.

The eldest, if I remember right, is not more than nine years of age; and they have advanced no farther in their education than being able to read English tolerably well. His Lordship's idea is, that when they shall have acquired a perfect knowledge of the French language, they may be taught Latin through the medium of that language, and pursue any other study that may be thought proper.

I have attended to his Lordship's objections against the public schools in England, and after due consideration, and weighing every circumstance, I remain of opinion, that no country but Great Britain is proper for the education of a British subject, who proposes to pass his life in his own country. The most important point, in my mind, to be secured in the education of a young man of rank of our country, is to make him an Englishman; and this can be done nowhere so effectually as in England.

He will there acquire those sentiments, that particular taste and turn of mind, which will make him prefer the government, and relish the manners, the diversions, and general way of living, which prevail in England.

He will there acquire that character, which distinguishes Englishmen from the natives of all the other countries of Europe, and which once attained, however it may be afterwards embellished or deformed, can never be entirely effaced.

If it could be proved, that this character is not the most amiable, it does not follow that it is not the most expedient. It is sufficient, that it is upon the whole most approved of in England. For I hold it as indisputable, that the good opinion of a man's countrymen is of more importance to him than that of all the rest of mankind: Indeed, without the first, he very rarely can enjoy the second.

It is thought, that, by an early foreign education, all ridiculous English prejudices will be avoided. This may be true;—but other prejudices, perhaps as ridiculous, and much more detrimental, will be formed. The first cannot be attended with many inconveniencies; the second may render the young people unhappy in their own country when they return, and disagreeable to their countrymen all the rest of their lives.

It is true, that the French manners are adopted in almost every country of Europe: they prevail all over Germany and the northern courts. They are gaining ground, though with a slower pace, in Spain, and in the Italian states.—This is not the case in England.—The English manners are universal in the provinces, prevail in the capital, and are to be found uncontaminated even at court.

In all the countries above mentioned, the body of the people behold this preference to foreign manners with disgust. But in all those countries, the sentiments of the people are disregarded; whereas, in England, popularity is of real importance; and the higher a man's rank is, the more he will feel the loss of it.

Besides, a prejudice against French manners is not confined to the lower ranks in England:—It is diffused over the whole nation. Even those who have none of the usual prejudices;—who do all manner of justice to the talents and ingenuity of their neighbours;—who approve of French manners in French people; yet cannot suffer them when grafted on their countrymen. Should an English gentleman think this kind of grafting at all admissible, it will be in some of the lowest classes with whom he is connected, as his tailor, barber, valet-de-chambre, or cook;—but never in his friend.

I can scarcely remember an instance of an Englishman of fashion, who has evinced in his dress or style of living a preference to French manners, who did not lose by it in the opinion of his countrymen.

What I have said of French manners is applicable to foreign manners in general, which are all in some degree French, and the particular differences are not distinguished by the English.

The sentiments of the citizens of Geneva are more analogous in many respects to the turn of thinking in England, than to the general opinions in France. Yet a Genevois in London will universally pass for a Frenchman.

An English boy, sent to Geneva at an early period of life, and remaining there six or seven years, if his parents be not along with him, will probably, in the eyes of the English, appear a kind of Frenchman all his life after. This is an inconvenience which ought to be avoided with the greatest attention.

With regard to the objections against public schools, they are in many respects applicable to those of every country. But I freely own, they never appeared to me sufficient to overbalance the advantages which attend that method of education; particularly as it is conducted in English public schools.

I have perceived a certain hardihood and manliness of character in boys who have had a public education, superior to what appears in those of the same age educated privately.

At a public school, though a general attention is paid to the whole, in many particulars each boy is necessitated to decide and act for himself. His reputation among his companions depends solely on his own conduct. This gradually strengthens the mind, inspires firmness and decision, and prevents that wavering imbecility observable in those who have been long accustomed to rely upon the assistance and opinion of others.

The original impressions which sink into the heart and mind, and form the character, never change.—The objects of our attention vary in the different periods of life.—This is sometimes mistaken for a change of character, which in reality remains essentially the same.—He who is reserved, deceitful, cruel, or avaricious, when a boy, will not, in any future period of life, become open, faithful, compassionate, or generous.

The young mind has, at a public school, the best chance of receiving those sentiments which incline the heart to friendship, and correct selfishness. They are drawn in by observation, which is infinitely more powerful than precept.

A boy perceives, that courage, generosity, gratitude, command the esteem and applause of all his companions. He cherishes these qualities in his own breast, and endeavours to connect himself in friendship with those who possess them.—He sees that meanness of spirit, ingratitude, and perfidy, are the objects of detestation.—He shuns the boys who display any indications of these odious qualities. What is the object of applause or contempt to his school-fellows, he will endeavour to graft into, or eradicate from, his own character, with ten thousand times more eagerness than that which was applauded and censured by his tutor or parents.

The admonitions of these last have probably lost their effect by frequent repetition; or he may imagine their maxims are only applicable to a former age, and to manners which are obsolete.—But he feels the sentiments of his companions affect his reputation and fame in the most sensible manner.

In all the countries of Europe, England excepted, such a deference is paid to boys of rank at the public schools, that emulation, the chief spur to diligence, is greatly blunted.—The boys in the middle rank of life are depressed by the insolence of their titled companions, which they are not allowed to correct or retaliate.—This has the worst effect on the minds of both, by rendering these more insolent, and those more abject.

The public schools in England disdain this mean partiality; and are, on that account, peculiarly useful to boys of high rank and great fortune. These young people are exceedingly apt to imbibe false ideas of their own importance, which in those impartial seminaries will be perfectly ascertained, and the real merit of the youths weighed in juster scales than are generally to be found in a parent's house.

The young peer will be taught by the matters, and still more effectually by his comrades, this most useful of all lessons,—to expect distinction and esteem from personal qualities only; because no other can make him estimable, or even save him from contempt.—He will see a dunce of high rank flogged with as little ceremony as the son of a tailor; and the richest coward kicked about by his companions equally with the poorest poltroon.—He will find that diligence, genius, and spirit, are the true sources of superiority and applause, both within and without the school.

The active principle of emulation, when allowed full play, as in the chief schools in England, operates in various ways, and always with a good effect.—If a boy finds that he falls beneath his companions in literary merit, he will endeavour to excel them in intrepidity, or some other accomplishment.—If he be brought to disgrace for neglecting his exercise, he will try to save himself from contempt by the firmness with which he bears his punishment.

The listlessness and indolence to be found so frequently among our young people of rank, are not to be imputed to their education at a public school, which in reality has the greatest tendency to counteract these habits, and often does so, and gives an energy to the mind which remains through life.

Those wretched qualities creep on afterwards, when the youths become their own masters, and have enfeebled their minds by indulging in all the pleasures which fortune puts in their power, and luxury presents.

Upon the whole, I am clearly of opinion, that the earliest period of every Englishman's education, during which the mind receives the most lasting impressions, ought to be in England.

If, however, the opinion of relations, or any peculiarity in situation, prevents his being educated at home, Geneva should be preferred to any other place. Or if, by some neglect, either of his own or his parents, a young English gentleman of fortune has allowed the first years of youth to fly unimproved, and has attained the age of seventeen or eighteen with little literary knowledge, I know no place where he may have a better chance of recovering what he has lost than in this city. He may have a choice of men of eminence, in every branch of literature, to assist him in his studies, a great proportion of whom are men of genius, and as amiable in their manners as they are eminent in their particular professions.

He will have constant opportunities of being in company with very ingenious people, whose thoughts and conversation turn upon literary subjects. In such society, a young man will feel the necessity of some degree of study. This will gradually form a taste for knowledge, which may remain through life.

It may also be numbered among the advantages of this place, that there are few objects of dissipation, and hardly any sources of amusement, besides those derived from the natural beauties of the country, and from an intimacy with a people by whose conversation a young man can scarce fail to improve.

P. S. An English nobleman and his lady having taken the resolution of educating their son at Geneva, attended him hither, and have effectually prevented the inconveniencies above mentioned, by remaining with him for seven or eight years.

The hospitality, generosity, and benevolent dispositions of this family had acquired them the highest degree of popularity. I saw them leave the place. Their carriage could with difficulty move through the multitude, who were assembled in the streets.—Numbers of the poorer sort, who had been relieved by their secret charity, unable longer to obey the injunctions of their benefactors, proclaimed their gratitude aloud.

The young gentleman was obliged to come out again and again to his old friends and companions, who pressed around the coach to bid him farewel, and express their sorrow for his departure, and their wishes for his prosperity. The eyes of the parents overflowed with tears of happiness; and the whole family carried along with them the affections of the greater part, and the esteem of all the citizens.

LETTER XXXII.

Geneva.

Suicide is very frequent at Geneva. I am told this has been the case ever since the oldest people in the republic can remember; and there is reason to believe, that it happens oftener here, in proportion to the number of inhabitants, than in England, or any other country of Europe.

The multiplicity of instances which has occurred since I have been here is astonishing. Two that have happened very lately are remarkable for the peculiar circumstances which accompanied them.

The first was occasioned by a sudden and unaccountable fit of despair, which seized the son of one of the wealthiest and most respectable citizens of the republic. This young gentleman had, in appearance, every reason to be satisfied with his lot. He was handsome, and in the vigour of youths married to a woman of an excellent character, who had brought him a great fortune, and by whom he was the father of a fine child. In the midst of all these blessings, surrounded by every thing which could inspire a man with an attachment to life, he felt it insupportable, and without any obvious cause of chagrin, determined to destroy himself.

Having passed some hours with his mother, a most valuable woman, and with his wife and child, he left them in apparent good humour, went into another room, applied the muzzle of a musket to his forehead, thrust back the trigger with his toe, and blew out his brains, in the hearing of the unsuspecting company he had just quitted.

The second instance, is that of a blacksmith, who, taking the same fatal resolution, and not having any convenient instrument at hand, charged an old gun-barrel with a brace of bullets, and putting one end into the fire of his forge, tied a string to the handle of the bellows, by pulling of which he could make them play, while he was at a convenient distance. Kneeling down, he then placed his head near the mouth of the barrel, and moving the bellows by means of the string, they blew up the fire, he keeping his head with astonishing firmness, and horrible deliberation, in that position, till the farther end of the barrel was so heated as to kindle the powder, whose explosion instantly drove the bullets through his brains.

Though I know that this happened literally as I have related, yet there is something so extraordinary, and almost incredible, in the circumstances, that perhaps I should not have mentioned it, had it not been well attested, and known to the inhabitants of Geneva, and all the English who are at present here.

Why suicide is more frequent in Great Britain and Geneva than elsewhere, would be a matter of curious investigation. For it appears very extraordinary, that men should be most inclined to kill themselves in countries where the blessings of life are best secured. There must be some strong and peculiar cause for an effect so preposterous.

Before coming here, I was of opinion, that the frequency of suicide in England was occasioned in a great measure by the stormy and unequal climate, which, while it clouds the sky, throws also a gloom over the minds of the natives.—To this cause, foreigners generally add, that of the use of coal, instead of wood, for fuel.

I rested satisfied with some vague theory, built on these taken together:—But neither can account for the same effect at Geneva, where coal is not used, and where the climate is the same with that in Switzerland, Savoy, and the neighbouring parts of France, where instances of suicide are certainly much more rare.

Without presuming to decide what are the remote causes of this fatal propensity, it appears evident to me, that no reasoning can have the smallest force in preventing it, but what is founded upon the soul's immortality and a future state.—What effect can the common arguments have on a man who does not believe that necessary and important doctrine?—He may be told, that he did not give himself life, therefore he has no right to take it away;—that he is a centinel on a post, and ought to remain till he is relieved;—what is all this to the man who thinks he is never to be questioned for his violence and desertion?

If you attempt to pique this man's pride, by asserting, that it is a greater proof of courage to bear the ills of life, than to flee from them; he will answer you from the Roman history, and ask, Whether Cato, Cassius, and Marcus Brutus, were cowards?

The great legislator of the Jews seems to have been convinced, that no law or argument against suicide could have any influence on the minds of people who were ignorant of the soul's immortality; and therefore, as he did not think it necessary to instruct them in the one (for reasons which the Bishop of Gloucester has unfolded in his treatise on the Divine Legation of Moses), he also thought it superfluous to give them any express law against the other.

Those philosophers, therefore, who have endeavoured to shake this great and important conviction from the minds of men, have thereby opened a door to suicide as well as to other crimes.—For, whoever reasons against that, without founding upon the doctrine of a future state, will soon see all his arguments overturned.

It must be acknowledged, indeed, that in many cases this question is decided by men's feelings, independent of reasonings of any kind.

Nature has not trusted a matter of so great importance entirely to the fallible reason of man; but has planted in the human breast such a love of life, and horror of death, as seldom can be overcome even by the greatest misfortunes.

But there is a disease which sometimes affects the body, and afterwards communicates its baneful influence to the mind, over which it hangs such a cloud of horrors as renders life absolutely insupportable. In this dreadful state, every pleasing idea is banished, and all the sources of comfort in life are poisoned.—Neither fortune, honours, friends, nor family, can afford the smallest satisfaction.—Hope, the last pillar of the wretched, falls to the ground—Despair lays hold of the abandoned sufferer—Then all reasoning becomes vain—Even arguments of religion have no weight, and the poor creature embraces death as his only friend, which, as he thinks, may terminate, but cannot augment, his misery.

I am, &c.

P. S. You need not write till you hear from me again, as I think it is probable that we shall have left this place before your letter could arrive.

LETTER XXXIII.

Lausanne.

The D—— of H—— having a desire to visit some of the German Courts, we bade adieu to our friends at Geneva, and are thus far on our intended journey. It is of peculiar advantage in Germany, above all other countries, to be in company with a man of rank and high title, because it facilitates your reception every where, and supersedes the necessity of recommendatory letters.

I have met here with my friend B——n, whose company and conversation have retarded our journey, by supplying the chief objects of travelling, if amusement and instruction are to be ranked among them. He is here with the M——s of L——y, a lively, spirited young man;—one of those easy, careless characters, so much beloved by their intimates, and so regardless of the opinion of the rest of mankind.

Since you hold me to my promise of writing so very regularly, you must sometimes expect to receive a letter dated from three or four different places, when either my short stay in one place deprives me of the leisure, or meeting with nothing uncommon in another deprives me of materials for so long a letter as you require.

The road from Geneva to this town is along the side of the lake, through a delightful country, abounding in vineyards, which produce the *vin de la côte*, so much esteemed. All the little towns on the way, Nyon, Rolle, and Morges, are finely situated, neatly built, and inhabited by a thriving and contented people.

Lausanne is the capital of this charming country, which formerly belonged to the Duke of Savoy, but is now under the dominion of the canton of Bern.

However mortifying this may be to the former possessor, it has certainly been a happy dispensation to the inhabitants of the Pays de Vaud, who are in every respect more at their ease, and in a better situation, than any of the subjects of his Sardinian Majesty.

This city is situated near the lake, and at the distance of about thirty miles from Geneva. As the nobility, from the country, and from some parts of Switzerland, and the families of several officers, who have retired from service, reside here, there is an air of more ease and gaiety (perhaps also more politeness) in the societies at Lausanne, than in those of Geneva; at least this is firmly believed and asserted by all the nobles of this place, who consider themselves as greatly superior to the citizens of Geneva. These, on the other hand, talk a good deal of the poverty, frivolousness, and ignorance of those same nobility, and make no scruple of ranking their own enlightened mechanics above them in every essential quality.

Vevay.

The road between Lausanne and Vevay is very mountainous; but the mountains are cultivated to the summits, and covered with vines.—This would have been impracticable on account of the steepness, had not the proprietors built strong stone-walls at proper intervals, one above the other, which support the soil, and form little terraces from the bottom to the top of the mountains.

The peasants ascend by narrow stairs, and, before they arrive at the ground they are to cultivate, have frequently to mount higher than a mason who is employed in repairing the top of a steeple.

The mountainous nature of this country subjects it to frequent torrents, which, when violent, sweep away vines, soil, and walls in one common destruction. The inhabitants behold the havoc with a steady concern, and, without giving way to the clamorous rage of the French, or sinking into the gloomy despair of the English, think only of the most effectual means of repairing the loss.—As soon as the storm has abated, they begin, with admirable patience and perseverance, to rebuild the walls, to carry fresh earth on hurdles to the top of the mountain, and to spread a new soil wherever the old has been washed away.

Where property is perfectly secure, and men allowed to enjoy the fruits of their own labour, they are capable of efforts unknown in those countries where despotism renders every thing precarious, and where a tyrant reaps what slaves have sown.

This part of the Pays de Vaud is inhabited by the descendents of those unhappy people, who were driven by the most absurd and cruel persecution from the vallies of Piedmont and Savoy.

I will not assert, that the iniquity of the persecutors has been visited upon their children; but the sufferings and stedfastness of the persecuted seem to be recompensed by the happy situation in which their children of the third and fourth generations are now placed.

Vevay is a pretty little town, containing between three and four thousand inhabitants. It is sweetly situated on a plain, near the head of the lake of Geneva, where the Rhone enters. The mountains behind the town, though exceedingly high, are entirely cultivated, like those on the road from Lausanne.

There is a large village about half-way up the mountain, in a direct line above Vevay, which, viewed from below, seems adhering to the side of the precipice, and has a very singular and romantic appearance.

The principal church is detached from the town, and situated on a hill which overlooks it. From the terrace, or church-yard, there is a view of the Alps, the Rhone, the lake, with towns and villages on its margin.—Within this church the body of General Ludlow is deposited. That steady republican withdrew from Lausanne to this place, after the assassination of his friend Lisle, who was shot through the heart, as he was going to church, by a ruffian, who had come across the lake for that purpose, and who, amidst the confusion occasioned by the murder, got safe to the boat, and escaped to the Duke of Savoy's territories on the other side, where he was openly protected.—This was a pitiful way of avenging the death of a monarch, who, whether justly or not, had been publicly condemned and executed.

There is a long Latin epitaph on Ludlow's monument, enumerating many circumstances of his life, but omitting the most remarkable of them all. He is called, Patriæ libertatis defensor, et potestatis arbitrariæ propugnator acerrimus, &c.—But no nearer hint is given of his having been one of King Charles the First's judges, and of his having signed the sentence against that ill-fated Prince.

However fond the Swiss in general may be of liberty, and however partial to its assertors, it is presumable that those who protected Ludlow, did not approve of this part of his story, and on that account a particular mention of it was not made on his tomb.

There is no travelling by post through Switzerland; we therefore hired horses at Geneva, to carry us to Basil; from whence we can proceed by post to Strasbourg, which is the route we design to take. We leave Lausanne the day after to-morrow.

LETTER XXXIV.

Bern.

On my return from Vevay to Lausanne, I found our friend, Mr. H―――y, at the inn, with the D――― of H―――. His Grace inclines to remain some time longer at that city; but desired that I might proceed with the carriages and all the servants, except his valet-de-chambre and one footman, to Strasbourg, which I readily agreed to, on his promising to join me there within a few days. H―――y, at the same time, made the very agreeable proposal of accompanying me to Strasbourg, where he will remain till our departure from thence, leaving his chaise for the D―――.

We began our journey the following day, and were escorted as far as Payerne by Messrs. B―――n and O―――n, where we passed a gay evening, and proceeded next morning to the town of Avanche, the capital of Switzerland in Tacitus's time[4].

No country in the world can be more agreeable to travellers during the summer than Switzerland: For, besides the commodious roads and comfortable inns, some of the most beautiful objects of nature, woods, mountains, lakes, intermingled with fertile fields, vineyards, and scenes of the most perfect cultivation, are here presented to the eye in greater variety, and on a larger scale, than in any other country.

From Avanche we advanced to Murten, or Murat, as it is pronounced by the French, a neat little town, situated upon a rising ground, on the side of the lake of the same name.

The army of Charles Duke of Burgundy, besieging this town, was defeated, with great slaughter, by the Swiss, in the year 1476. Near the road, within a mile of Murat, there is a little building full of human bones, which are said to be those of the Burgundians slain in that battle. As this curious cabinet was erected many years after the battle, it may be supposed, that some of the bones of the victors are here packed up along with those of the vanquished, in order to swell the collection.

There are several inscriptions on the chapel.

DEO OPTIM. MAX.
CAROLI INCLITI ET FORTISSIMI BURGUNDIÆ DUCIS
EXERCITUS MURATUM OBSIDENS AB HELVETIIS
CÆSUS HOC SUI MONUMENTUM RELIQUIT, 1476

On another side is the following:

SACELLUM
QUO RELIQUIAS
EXERCITUS BURGUNDICI
AB HELVETIIS, A. 1476,
PIA ANTIQUITAS CONDIDIT.
RENOVARI
VIISQUE PUBLICIS MUNIRI
JUSSERUNT
RERUM NUNC DOMINÆ
REIPUBLICÆ
BERNENSIS ET FRIBURGENSIS
ANNO 1755.

The borders of the lake of Murat are enriched with gentlemen's houses, and villages in great abundance.

The dress, manners, and persons of the inhabitants of this country indicate a different people from the Genevois, Savoyards, or the inhabitants of the Pays de Vaud.

We dined at Murat, and remained several hours in the town. There was a fair, and a great concourse of people.—The Swiss peasants are the tallest and most robust I have ever seen. Their dress is very particular.—They have little round hats, like those worn by the Dutch skippers.—Their coats and waistcoats are all of a kind of coarse black cloth.—Their breeches are made of coarse linen, something like sailors trowsers; but drawn together in plaits below the knees, and the stockings are of the same stuff with the breeches.

The women wear short jackets, with a great superfluity of buttons. The unmarried women value themselves on the length of their hair, which they separate into two divisions, and allow to hang at its full length, braided with ribands in the Ramillie fashion.—After marriage, these tresses are no longer permitted to hang down; but, being twisted round the head in spiral lines, are fixed at the crown with large silver pins. This is the only difference in point of dress which matrimony makes.

Married and unmarried wear straw hats, ornamented with black ribands. So far the women's dress is becoming enough; but they have an aukward manner of fixing their petticoats so high as to leave hardly any waist. This encroachment of the petticoats upon the waist, with the amazing number they wear, gives a size and importance to the lower and hind part of the body to which it is by no means entitled, and mightily deforms the appearance of the whole person.

The elegant figure of the Venus de Medicis, or of the D———ss of D———re, would be impaired, or annihilated, under such a preposterous load of dress.—As we arrived only this afternoon, I can say nothing of Bern. You shall hear more in my next. Meanwhile, I am, &c.

[4] Near this town the Helvetians were defeated by Cæcina, one of Vitellius's Lieutenants.—Multa hominum millia cæsa, multa sub corona venumdata. Cumque direptis omnibus, Aventicum gentis caput justo agmine peteretur.

Taciti Historia, lib. 1. cap. 68.

LETTER XXXV.

Bern.

Bern is a regular well-built town, with some air of magnificence. The houses are of a fine white free-stone, and pretty uniform, particularly in the principal street, where they are all exactly of the same height. There are piazzas on each side, with a walk, raised four feet above the level of the street, very commodious in wet weather.

A small branch of the Aar has been turned into this street, and being confined to a narrow channel in the middle, which has a considerable slope, it runs with great rapidity; and, without being a disagreeable object of itself, is of great service in keeping the street clean.

Another circumstance contributes to render this one of the most cleanly towns in Europe:—Criminals are employed in removing rubbish from the streets and public walks. The more atrocious delinquents are chained to waggons, while those who are condemned for smaller crimes, are employed in sweeping the light rubbish into the rivulet, and throwing the heavier into the carts or waggons, which their more criminal companions are obliged to push or draw along.

These wretches have collars of iron fixed around their necks, with a projecting handle in the form of a hook to each, by which, on the slightest offence or mutiny, they may be seized, and are entirely at the command of the guard, whose duty it is to see them perform their work.—People of both sexes are condemned to this labour for months, years, or for life, according to the nature of their crimes.

It is alleged, that over and above the deterring from crimes, which is effected by this, in common with the other methods of punishing, there is the additional advantage, of obliging the criminal to repair by his labour the injury which he has done to the community.

I suspect, however, that this advantage is overbalanced by the bad effects of habituating people to behold the misery of their fellow-creatures, which I imagine gradually hardens the hearts of the spectators, and renders them less susceptible of the emotions of compassion and pity;—feelings, which, perhaps of all others, have the best influence upon, and are the most becoming, human nature. Juvenal says,

—— mollissima corda

Humano generi dare se natura fatetur,

Quæ lachrymas dedit: hæc nostri pars optima sensûs.

Wherever public executions and punishments are frequent, the common people have been observed to acquire a greater degree of insensibility, and cruelty of disposition, than in places where such scenes seldom occur.—I remember, while I was at Geneva, where executions are very rare, a young man was condemned to be hanged for murder, and there was a general gloom and uneasiness evident in every society for several days before and after the execution.

The public buildings at Bern, as the hospital, the granary, the guard-house, the arsenal, and the churches, are magnificent. There is a very elegant building just completed, with accommodations for many public amusements, such as balls, concerts, and theatrical entertainments. There are also apartments for private societies and assemblies. It was built by a voluntary subscription among the nobility; and no societies, but of the patrician order, are allowed there.

Theatrical entertainments are seldom permitted at Bern; none have as yet been performed at this new theatre.

The walk by the great church was formerly the only public walk, and much admired on account of the view from it, and the peculiarity of its situation, being on a level with the streets on one side, and some hundred feet of perpendicular height above them on the other. But there is now another public walk, at some distance without the town, which has been lately made upon a high bank by the side of the Aar, and is the most magnificent I ever saw belonging to this or any other town. From it there is a commanding view of the river, the town of Bern, the country about it, and the Glaciers of Switzerland.

I have visited the library, where, besides the books, there are a few antiques, and some other curiosities. The small figure of the priest pouring wine between the horns of a bull, is valuable only because it illustrates a passage in Virgil, and has been mentioned by Addison.

An addition was lately made to this library by a collection of English books, magnificently bound, which were sent as a present by an English gentleman; who, though he has thought proper to conceal his name, has sufficiently discovered his political principles by the nature of the collection, amongst which, I distinguished Milton's works, particularly his prose writings;

Algernon Sidney on Government, Locke, Ludlow's Memoirs, Gordon's translation of Tacitus, Addison's works, particularly The Freeholder; Marvel's works, Steel's, &c. They were the largest and finest editions, and might be about the value of 200l.—This gentleman made a present of the same nature to the public library at Geneva.

I happened to open the Glasgow edition of Homer, which I saw here, on a blank page of which was an address in Latin to the Corsican General, Paoli, signed James Boswell. This very elegant book had been sent, I suppose, as a present from Mr. Boswell to his friend the General; and, when that unfortunate chief was obliged to abandon his country, fell, with other of his effects, into the hands of the Swiss officer in the French service, who made a present of the Homer to this library.

The arsenal I could not have omitted seeing had I been so inclined, as the Bernois value themselves on the trophies contained in it, and upon the quantity, good condition, and arrangement of the arms.

Nothing interested me so much as the figures of the brave Switzers, who first took arms against tyranny, and that of William Tell, who is represented aiming at the apple on his son's head. I contemplated this with an emotion which was created by the circumstances of the story, not by the workmanship; for, at that moment, I should have beheld with neglect the most exquisite statue that ever was formed of Augustus Cæsar.

Surely no characters have so just a claim to the admiration and gratitude of posterity, as those who have freed their countrymen from the capricious insolence of tyrants: And whether all the incidents of Tell's story be true or fabulous, the men (whoever they were) who roused and incited their fellow-citizens to throw off the Austrian yoke, deserve to be regarded as patriots, having undoubtedly been actuated by that principle, so dear to every generous heart, the spirit of independence,

> "Who with the gen'rous rustics fate,
>
> "On Uri's rock, in close divan,
>
> "And wing'd that arrow sure as fate,
>
> "Which ascertain'd the sacred rights of man."

Mr. Addison observes, that there is no great pleasure in visiting arsenals, merely to see a repetition of these magazines of war; yet it is worth while, as it gives an idea of the force of a state, and serves to fix in the mind the most considerable parts of its history.

The arms taken from the Burgundians, in the various battles which established the liberty of Switzerland, are displayed here; also the figure of the General of Bern, who, in the year 1536, conquered the Pays de Vaud from Charles III. Duke of Savoy:—And, if they have no trophies to shew of a later date, I am convinced it is because they are too poor and too wise to aim at any extension of dominion:—And because all the neighbouring powers are at length become sensible, that the nature of their country, and their personal valour, have rendered the Swiss as unconquerable, as, from political considerations, they are averse to attempt conquests.

LETTER XXXVI.

Bern.

The different cantons of Switzerland, though united together by a common bond, and all of a republican form of government, differ in the nature of that form, as well as in religion.

The Roman Catholic religion being favourable to monarchy, one would naturally imagine, that, when adopted by a republic, it would gradually wind up the government to the highest pitch of aristocracy.

The fact nevertheless is, that those cantons, which are in the strongest degree democratical, are of the Popish persuasion; and the most perfect aristocracy of them all is established in this Protestant canton of Bern, which is also indeed the most powerful. In extent of country, and number of inhabitants, it is reckoned nearly equal to all the others taken together.

The nobility of Bern are accused of an extraordinary degree of pride and stateliness. They affect to keep the citizens at a great distance; and it is with difficulty that their wives and daughters will condescend to mix with the mercantile families at balls, assemblies, and such public occasions, where numbers seem essential to the nature of the entertainment; by which means a nobility ball loses in cheerfulness what it retains in dignity, and is often, as I am told, as devoid of amusement as it is solemn.

The whole power of the government, and all the honourable offices of the state, are in the hands of the nobility. As it is not permitted them to trade, they would naturally fall into poverty without this resource: But by the number of places which the nobles enjoy, and to which very considerable pensions are annexed, the poorest of them are enabled to support their families with dignity.

The bailliages, into which the whole canton and the conquered territories are divided, form lucrative and honourable establishments for the principal families of Bern. The bailiff is governor and judge in his own district, and there is a magnificent chateau in each for his accommodation. An appeal may be made from all subordinate courts to him; as also from his decision, to the council at Bern.

The nobility of Bern, though born to be judges, are not always instructed in law. It has therefore been thought requisite, to appoint a certain number of persons, as their assessors, who have been bred to the profession. But in case the judge should differ from those assessors, and retain his own opinion in spite of their remonstrances, as nobility has the precedency of law, the decision must be given according to the will of the judge.

This office remains in the hands of the same person for the term of six years only. I have been informed, that in some of these bailliages, the governor may live with proper magnificence, and lay up, during the period of his office, two or three thousand pounds, without extortion, or unbecoming parsimony. There is no law against his being afterwards named to another bailliage.

The executive power of the government, with all the lucrative and honourable offices, being thus in the hands of the nobility, it may be imagined, that the middle and lower ranks of people are poor and oppressed. This, however, is by no means the case; for the citizens, I mean the merchants and trades-people, seem, in general, to enjoy all the comforts and conveniencies of life. And the peasantry is uncommonly wealthy throughout the whole canton of Bern.

The Swiss have no objection to their nobles being their judges, and to the principal offices of government remaining in their hands. They look upon the nobility as their natural superiors, and think, that they and their families ought to be supported with a certain degree of splendor:—But the power of direct taxation is a different question, and must be managed with all possible caution and delicacy. It is a common cause, and the conduct of the nobles in this particular is watched with very jealous eyes. They are sufficiently aware of this, and use their power with moderation. But lest the nobles should at any time forget, a very good hint is given in a German inscription in the arsenal, implying, That the insolence and rapacity of high rank had brought about the liberty of Switzerland.

A people who have always arms in their hands, and form the only military force of the country, are in no danger of being oppressed and irritated with taxes.

It has been considered by some as a pernicious policy in the Swiss, to allow so many of their inhabitants to serve as mercenaries in the different armies of Europe. There are others, who consider this measure as expedient, or less pernicious in the Swiss cantons, than it would be in any other country.

They who support this opinion, assert, that every part of Switzerland, which is capable of cultivation, is already improved to the highest degree; that, after retaining a sufficient number of hands to keep it always in this condition, and for the support of every manufactory, still there remains a surplus of inhabitants, which forms the troops that are allowed to go into foreign services. They add, that these troops only engage for a limited number of years, after the expiration of which, many of them return with money to their native country; and all of them, by stipulation, may be recalled by the state on any emergency.—By this means, they retain a numerous and well-disciplined army on foot; which, so far from being a burden, in reality enriches the state:—an advantage which no other people ever possessed.

There is still another motive for this measure, which, though it be not openly avowed, yet, I suspect, has considerable weight: The council are perhaps afraid, that if the young nobility were kept at home, where they could have but few objects to occupy them, they might cabal and spread dissentions in the state; or perhaps, through idleness and ambition, excite dangerous insurrections among the peasants. For, although the laws are severe against state crimes, and easily put in execution against ordinary offenders, it might be difficult and dangerous to punish a popular young nobleman.

It may on these accounts be thought highly prudent, to allow a large proportion of them to exhaust, in some foreign service, the fiery and restless years of youth, which at home might have been spent in faction and dangerous intrigues. Very probably the states would incline to permit the officers to go, while they retained the private men at home; but are under a necessity of allowing the latter also, because without them the officers could not be raised to those distinguished situations in foreign services which are their greatest inducements to leave their own country.

After having served a certain time, almost all of them return to Switzerland. Some, because they are tired of dissipation; others to inherit a paternal estate; and many with pensions from the Princes they have served.—The heat of youth is then most probably over.—They begin to aspire to those offices in their own country to which their birth gives them a claim, and which they now prefer to the lustre of military rank. They wish to support those laws, and that government, which they find so partial to their families; or they desire to pass the remainder of life in ease and retirement on their paternal estates.

It is remarkable, that the Swiss officers, who return from foreign services, particularly that of France, instead of importing French manners to their native mountains, and infecting their countrymen with the luxuries and fopperies of that nation, throw off all foreign airs with their uniform, and immediately resume the plain and frugal style of life which prevails in their own country.

LETTER XXXVII.

Basil.

Having, on a former occasion, made a more extensive tour through Switzerland, we determined not to deviate from the direct road to Strasbourg. In pursuance of this resolution, H——y and I, when we left Bern, passed by Soleurre, the capital of the canton of the same name.

Soleurre is an agreeable little town situated on the river Aar. The houses are neatly built, and not inelegant; the meanest of them have a cleanly appearance. The common people seem to be in easier circumstances, and have a greater air of content, than in any Roman Catholic country I have ever visited. The inn where we lodged has the comfortable look of an English one. The French ambassador to the cantons has his residence in this town. One of the churches of Soleurre is the most magnificent modern building in Switzerland.

The arsenal is stored with arms in proportion to the number of inhabitants in the canton; and there are trophies, and other monuments of the valour of their ancestors, as in the arsenal of Bern. In the middle of the hall there are thirteen figures of men in complete armour, representing the thirteen Swiss cantons.

The country between Soleurre and Basil, though very hilly, is beautiful, perhaps the more so on that account; because of the variety of surface and different views it presents. H——y and I had more leisure to admire those fine landscapes than we wished, for the axle tree of the chaise broke at some miles distant from Basil.

It was the gay season of the vintage.—The country was crowded with peasantry of both sexes and every age, all employed in gathering and carrying home the grapes. Our walk for these few miles was agreeable and amusing. In all countries this is the season of joy and festivity, and approaches nearest the exaggerated description which the ancient poets have given of rural happiness. Perhaps there is in reality not so much exaggeration in their description, as alteration in our manners.—For, if the peasants were allowed to enjoy the fruits of their own labour, would not their lives be more delightful than those of any other people?—In spite of poverty and oppression, a happy enthusiasm, a charming madness, and perfect oblivion of care, are diffused all over France during the vintage.—Every village is enlivened with music, dancing, and glee;—and were it not for their tattered clothes and emaciated countenances, one who viewed them in the vintage season, would imagine the country people of France in a situation as enviable as that which, according to the Poets, was formerly enjoyed by the Shepherds of Arcadia.—The peasantry of this country have not so great a sensibility or expression of joy; and though blessed with health, freedom, and abundance, a composed satisfaction, a kind of phlegmatic good-humour, mark the boundaries of their happiness.

When we arrived at Basil, we went directly to the Three Kings. This inn, in point of situation, is the most agreeable you can well imagine. The Rhine washes its walls, and the windows of a large dining-room look across that noble river to the fertile plains on the opposite side.

I am just returned from that same dining-room, where H——y and I thought proper to sup.—There were ten or a dozen people at table.—I sat next to a genteel-looking man from Strasbourg, with whom I conversed a good deal during supper. He had for his companion a round-faced, rosy, plump gentleman, from Amsterdam, who did not speak French; but the Strasburgher addressed him from time to time in Low Dutch, to which the other replied by nods.

When the retreat of the greater part of the company had contracted the little circle which remained, I expressed some regret to my Strasbourg acquaintance, that Mr. H——y and I could not speak a little Dutch; or that his friend could not speak French, that we might enjoy the pleasure of his conversation. This was immediately translated to the Dutchman, who heard it with great composure, and then took his pipe from his mouth, and made an answer, which I got our interpreter, with some difficulty, to explain. It was to this effect:—That we ought to console ourselves for the accident of our not understanding each other; for as we had no connection, or dealings in trade together, our conversing could not possibly answer any useful purpose. H——y made a low bow to this compliment, saying, that the justness and good sense of that remark had certainly escaped my observation, as he acknowledged it had hitherto done his.

A man that travels, you see, my friend, and takes care to get into good company, is always learning something.—Had I not visited the Three Kings at Basil, I might have conversed all my lifetime without knowing the true use of language.

LETTER XXXVIII.

Basil.

There has been an interval of three days since I had the conversation with my ingenious acquaintance from Amsterdam. We are assured that the chaise, which has been accommodated with a new axle-tree, will be ready this afternoon. In the interim, I shall write you a few remarks on this town.

Basil is larger than any town in Switzerland, but not so populous for its size as Geneva. The inhabitants seem to be uncommonly afraid of thieves, most of the windows being guarded by iron bars or grates, like those of convents or prisons.

I observed at the lower end of many windows a kind of wooden box, projecting towards the street, with a round glass, of about half a foot diameter, in the middle. I was told this was for the conveniency of people within; who, without being seen, choose to sit at the windows, and amuse themselves by looking at the passengers;—that they were mostly occupied by the ladies, who are taught to think it indecent to appear at the windows.

The inhabitants of Basil seem to be of a reserved and saturnine disposition; whether it is natural or affected I cannot tell, but the few I conversed with, had something uncommonly serious and formal in their manner. How an unremitting gravity and solemnity of manner in the common affairs of life, comes to be considered as an indication of wisdom, or of extraordinary parts, is what I never could understand.—So many ridiculous things occur every day in this world, that men who are endowed with that degree of sensibility which usually accompanies genius, find it very difficult to maintain a continued gravity. This difficulty is abundantly felt even in the grave and learned professions of law, physic, and divinity; and the individuals who have been most successful in surmounting it, and who never deviate from the solemnity of established forms, have not always been the most distinguished for real knowledge or genius; though they generally are most admired by the multitude, who are very apt to mistake that gravity for wisdom, which proceeds from a literal weight of brain, and muddiness of understanding. Mistakes of the same kind are frequently made in forming a judgment of books, as well as men. Those which profess a formal design to instruct and reform, and carry on the work methodically till the reader is lulled into repose, have passed for deep and useful performances; while others, replete with original observation and real instruction, have been treated as frivolous, because they are written in a familiar style, and the precepts conveyed in a sprightly and indirect manner.

Works which are composed with the laborious desire of being thought profound, have so very often the misfortune to be dull, that some people have considered the two terms as synonymous; and the men who receive it as a rule, that one set of books are profound because they are dull, may naturally conclude that others are superficial because they are entertaining. With respect to books, however, matters are soon set to rights; those of puffed and false pretensions die neglected, while those of real merit live and flourish. But with regard to the men, the catastrophe is often different; we daily see formal assuming blockheads flourish and enjoy the fruits of their pompous impositions, while many men of talents who disdain such arts, live in obscurity, and die neglected.—I ask you pardon, I have just recollected that I was giving you some account of Basil.

The library here is much esteemed.—It is reckoned particularly rich in manuscripts. They showed us one of a Greek New Testament, with which you may believe H——y and I were greatly edified. We are told it is above a thousand years old.

At the arsenal is shown, the armour in which Charles Duke of Burgundy was killed. That unfortunate prince has ornamented all the arsenals in Switzerland with trophies.

We visited the hall where the famous Council sat so many years, and voted so intrepidly against the Pope. Not satisfied with condemning his conduct, they actually damned him in effigy. A famous painting, in the town-house, is supposed to have been executed under their auspices. In this piece the Devil is represented driving the Pope and several ecclesiastics before him to Hell.—Why they should suppose the Devil should be so very active against his Holiness, I know no reason.

Here are many pictures of Hans Holben's (who was a native of Basil, and the favourite painter of Henry VIII. to whom he was first recommended by Erasmus); particularly, several portraits of Erasmus, and one sketch of Sir Thomas More's family. Though portraits are in general the most insipid of all kinds of paintings, yet those of such celebrated persons, done by such a painter, are certainly very interesting pieces.

The most admired of all Holben's works, is a suite of small pieces in different compartments, representing the passion and sufferings of our Saviour. In these the colours remain with wonderful vivacity.

We were also conducted to the dismal gallery, upon whose walls, what is called Holben's Death's Dance, is represented. The colours having been long exposed to the air, are now quite faded, which I can scarce think is much to be regretted, for the plan of the piece is so wretched, that the finest execution could hardly prevent it from giving disgust.

A skeleton, which represents Death, leads off, in a dancing attitude, people of both sexes, of all ages, and of every condition, from the emperor to the beggar. All of them display the greatest unwillingness to accompany their hideous partner, who, regardless of tears, expostulations, and bribes, draws them along.

You will take notice, that there is a Death for each character, which occasions a nauseous repetition of the same figure; and the reluctance marked by the different people who are forced to this hated minuet, is in some accompanied with grimaces so very ridiculous, that one cannot refrain from smiling, which surely is not the effect the painter intended to produce.—If he did, of all the contrivances that ever were thought of to put people in good-humour, his must be allowed the most extraordinary.

To this piece, such as it is, Prior alludes in his ode to the memory of Colonel Villers.

> Nor aw'd by foresight, nor misled by chance,
>
> Imperious Death directs his ebon lance,
>
> Peoples great Henry's tomb, and leads up Holben's dance.

In this city all the clocks are an hour advanced. When it is but one o'clock in all the towns and villages around, it is exactly two at Basil. This singularity is of three or four hundred years standing; and what is as singular as the custom itself, the origin of it is not known. This is plain, by their giving quite different accounts of it.

The most popular story is, that, about four hundred years ago, the city was threatened with an assault by surprise. The enemy was to begin the attack when the large clock of the tower at one end of the bridge should strike one after midnight. The artist who had the care of the clock, being informed that this was the expected signal, caused the clock to be altered, and it struck two instead of one; so the enemy thinking they were an hour too late, gave up the attempt; and in commemoration of this deliverance, all the clocks in Basil have ever since struck two at one o'clock, and so on.

In case this account of the matter should not be satisfactory, they show, by way of confirmation, a head, which is placed near to this patriotic clock, with the face turned to the road by which the enemy was to have entered. This same head lolls out its tongue every minute, in the most insulting manner possible. This was originally a piece of mechanical wit of the famous clockmaker's who saved the town. He framed it in derision of the enemy, whom he had so dexterously deceived. It has been repaired, renewed, and enabled to thrust out its tongue every minute, for these four hundred years, by the care of the magistrates, who think so excellent a joke cannot be too often repeated.

LETTER XXXIX.

Strasbourg.

Nothing can form a finer contrast with the mountains of Switzerland than the plains of Alsace. From Basil to Strasbourg, is a continued, well cultivated plain, as flat almost as a bowling-green. We saw great quantities of tobacco hanging at the peasants doors, as we came along, this herb being plentifully cultivated in these fields.

We have passed some days very agreeably in this town. One can scarcely be at a loss for good company and amusement, in a place where there is a numerous French garrison. Marechal Contades resides here at present, as commander of the troops, and governor of the province. He lives in a magnificent manner. The English who happen to pass this way, as well as the officers of the garrison, have great reason to praise his hospitality and politeness.

After dining at his house, with several English gentlemen, he invited the company to his box at the playhouse. Voltaire's Enfant Prodigue was acted; and for the Petite Pièce, le François à Londres. Our nation is a little bantered, as you know, in the last. The eyes of the spectators were frequently turned towards the Marechal's box, to observe how we bore the raillery. We clapped heartily, and showed the most perfect good-humour. There was indeed no reason to do otherwise. The satire is genteel, and not too severe; and reparation is made for the liberties taken; for in the same piece, all manner of justice is done to the real good qualities belonging to the English national character.

An old French officer, who was in the next box to us, seemed uneasy, and hurt at the peals of laughter which burst from the audience at some particular passages: he touched my shoulder, and assured me that no nation was more respected in France than the English;—adding, 'Hanc veniam damus, petimusque vicissim.'

It were to be wished that French characters, when brought on the English stage, had been always treated with as little severity, and with equal justice; and not so often sacrificed to the illiberal and absurd prejudices of the vulgar.

I have seen the greater number of the regiments perform their exercise separately, and there has been one general field-day since I came hither. The French troops are infinitely better clothed, and in all respects better appointed than they were during the last war. For this reformation, I am told they are obliged to the Duc de Choiseul, who, though now in disgrace, still retains many friends in the army.

There are, besides the French, two German regiments in this garrison. These admit of the discipline of the cane upon every slight occasion, which is never permitted among the French troops. Notwithstanding their being so plentifully provided with those severe flappers to rouse their attention, I could not perceive that the German regiments went through their exercise with more precision or alertness than the French; and any difference would, in my opinion, be dearly purchased at the price of treating one soldier like a spaniel.

Perhaps what improves the hardy and phlegmatic German, would have a contrary effect on the more delicate and lively Frenchman; as the same severity which is requisite to train a pointer, would render a greyhound good for nothing.

After all, I question very much whether this shocking custom is absolutely necessary in the armies of any nation; for, let our martinets say what they please, there is surely some difference between men and dogs.

With respect to the French, I am convinced that great severity would break their spirit, and impair that fire and impetuosity in attack, for which they have been distinguished, and which makes French troops more formidable than any other quality they possess.

I must own I was highly pleased with the easy, familiar air, and appearance of good will, with which the French officers in general speak to the common soldiers.—This, I am told, does not diminish the respect and obedience which soldiers owe to their superiors, or that degree of subordination which military discipline exacts. On the contrary, it is asserted, that to these properties, which the French possess in common with other soldiers, they join a kind of grateful attachment and affection.

In some services, the behaviour of the officers to the private soldiers is so morose, severe, and unrelenting, that a man might be led to believe that one of their principal enjoyments was to render the lives of the common men as miserable as possible.

If a certain degree of gentleness does no harm in the great articles of obedience and subordination, it is surely worth while to pay some attention to the feelings of so large a proportion of mankind, as are by modern policy necessitated to follow a military life. To put *their* happiness entirely out of the question, in the government of the armies of which they form infinitely the major part, is rather hard treatment of creatures who are of the same species, employed in the same cause, and exposed to the same dangers with their officers.

When I began this, I intended to have told you a few things about Strasbourg, instead of which I have been led out of my way by French and German soldiers.—Digressing is a trick to which I am very subject, and rather than not be indulged in it, I would throw away my pen altogether.

The D—— of H—— arrived here exactly at the time he proposed.

LETTER XL.

Strasbourg.

The cathedral of Strasbourg is a very fine building, and never fails to attract the attention of strangers.

Our Gothic ancestors, like the Greeks and Romans, built for posterity. Their ideas in architecture, though different from those of the Grecian artists, were vast, sublime, and generous, far superior to the selfish snugness of modern taste, which is generally confined to one or two generations; the plans of our ancestors with a more extensive benevolence embrace distant ages. Many Gothic buildings still habitable evince this, and ought to inspire sentiments of gratitude to those who have not grudged such labour and expence for the accommodation of their remote posterity.

The number and magnitude of Gothic churches, in the different countries of Europe, form a presumption, that the clergy were not devoid of public spirit in those days; for if the powerful ecclesiastics had then been entirely actuated by motives of self-interest, they would have turned the excessive influence which they had acquired over the minds of their fellow-citizens, to purposes more immediately advantageous to themselves; instead of encouraging them to raise magnificent churches for the use of the public, they might have preached it up as still more meritorious to build fine houses and palaces for the immediate servants and ambassadors of God.—But we find very few ecclesiastical palaces, in comparison with the number of churches which still remain for the public conveniency. This sufficiently shows the injustice of those indiscriminating satirists, who assert that the clergy in all ages and countries have displayed a spirit equally proud and interested.

No species of architecture is better contrived for the dwelling of *heavenly pensive contemplation*, than the Gothic; it has a powerful tendency to fill the mind with sublime, solemn, and religious sentiments; the antiquity of the Gothic churches contributes to increase that veneration which their form and size inspire. We naturally feel a respect for a fabric into which we know that our forefathers have entered with reverence, and which has stood the assaults of many centuries, and of a thousand storms. That religious melancholy which usually possesses the mind in large Gothic churches, is however considerably counteracted by certain satirical bas reliefs with which the pillars and cornices of this church of Strasbourg was originally ornamented.—The vices of monks are here exposed under the allegorical figure of hogs, asses, monkies, and foxes, which being dressed in monkish habits, perform the most venerable functions of religion. And for the edification of those who do not comprehend allegory, a monk in the robes of his order, is engraved on the pulpit in a most indecent posture, with a nun lying by him.

Upon the whole, the cathedral of Strasbourg is considered by some people as the most impious, and by others as the merriest Gothic church in Christendom. I leave you to solve the problem as you please.—As for me, I am a very unconcerned passenger.

I say nothing of the great clock and its various movements. Though it was an object of admiration when first constructed, it is beheld with indifference by modern artists.

I had the curiosity to ascend the steeple of this cathedral, which is reckoned one of the highest in Europe, its height being 574 feet. You may easily form an idea of the view from it, when I tell you it comprehends the town of Strasbourg, the extensive plains of Alsace, with the Rhine flowing through them. Such views are not uncommon: They are always agreeable, but do not astonish and elevate the mind, like the wild, irregular, and sublime scenes in Switzerland.

One forenoon as I was sauntering through the streets with some of our countrymen, we were informed that the music of some of the regiments had been ordered to a particular church, where the Count de ———, son of Lewis the XVth by Madam de Pompadour, was expected to be at mass.—We all immediately went for the sake of the military music, and found a very numerous and genteel company attending. After having waited a considerable time, it struck twelve, upon which the whole company retired, without hearing the music or mass.—After mid-day the ceremony could not have been performed, although the Count had come. Something very important must have intervened to prevent a Frenchman, and one of his character for politeness, from attending on such an occasion. There was however a murmur of disapprobation for this want of attention, and the priest was not applauded, who had hazarded the souls of a whole churchful of people, out of complaisance to one man; for those who imagine that a mass can save souls, must admit that the want of it may be the cause of damnation. Mr. H———y whispered me, "In England they would not have had half the complaisance for the king himself, accompanied by all his legitimate children, that these people have shewn to this son of a w———e."

To indemnify myself for this disappointment, I went the same afternoon with a French officer to hear a celebrated preacher. The subject of his discourse was the miserable situation of men who were under the dominion of their passions.—Do you wish for a sample of his discourse?—Here it is:—

"A slave in the galleys (cried the preacher) is happier, and more free, than a man under the tyranny of his passions; for though the body of the slave is in chains, his mind may be free.—Whereas the wretch who is under the government of his passions, has his mind, his very soul, in chains.—Is his passion lust?—He will sacrifice a faithful servant to gratify it;—David did so. Is it avarice?—he will betray his master;—Judas did so.—Is he attached to a mistress?—he will murder a saint to please her;—Herod did so."

As we returned from the church, the French officer, who had been for some time in a reverie, said, Ma foi, cet homme parle avec beaucoup d'onction; je vais profiter de son sermon.—Où est-ce que vous allez? said I.—Je m'en vais chez Nanette, replied he, pour me débarrasser de ma passion dominante.

Among the curiosities of the cathedral, I ought to have mentioned two large bells, which they show to strangers. One is of brass, and weighs ten tons; the other of silver, which they say weighs above two.—They also show a large French horn, whose history is as follows.—About four hundred years ago, the Jews formed a conspiracy to betray the city, and with this identical horn, they intended to give the enemy notice when to begin the attack.

Is it not amazing that such a number of strange stories have been circulated concerning these same Jews?

The plot, however, was discovered; many of the Jews were burnt alive, the rest were plundered of their money and effects, and banished the town. And this horn is sounded twice every night from the battlements of the steeple in gratitude for the deliverance.

The Jews, as you would expect, deny every circumstance of this story, except the murdering and pillaging their countrymen. They say the whole story was fabricated to furnish a pretext for these robberies and murders, and assert that the steeple of Strasbourg, as has been said of the monument of London,

"Like a tall bully lifts the head and lies."

LETTER XLI.

Manheim.

All the advantages I might propose from the D—— of H——'s company, did not prevent my regret at parting from my friend H——y, who set out for Lyons the same morning on which we left Strasbourg.

Upon crossing the Rhine we entered into the territories of the Margrave of Baden Durlach, which lie along the banks of that river immediately opposite to Alsace.

At Rastade we were informed that the Margrave and his family were at Karlsruch. Rastade is the capital of this prince's dominions.—The town is but small, and not very populous:—The Margrave's palace, however, is sufficiently large.—We made only a short stay to examine it, being impatient to get on to Karlsruch.

There is another very magnificent palace at Karlsruch, built in good taste. It was begun many years ago, and has been lately finished by the reigning prince.

The town of Karlsruch is built on a regular plan. It consists of one principal street of above an English mile in length. This street is at a considerable distance in front of the palace, and in a parallel direction with it. All the other streets go off at different angles from the principal one, in such a manner as that whichsoever of them you enter, walking from it, the view is terminated by the front of the palace. The length of these smaller streets is ascertained, none of them being allowed to encroach on the spacious area, which is kept clear before the palace.

The principal street may be extented to any length, and as many additional streets as they please may be built from it, all of which, according to this plan, will have the palace for a termination.

The houses of this town are all as uniform as the streets, being of an equal size and height; so that one would be led to imagine that none of the inhabitants are in any considerable degree richer or poorer than their neighbours. There are indeed a few new houses, more elegant than the others, belonging to some of the officers of the court, built at one side of the palace; but they are not, properly speaking, in the town.

Having announced in the usual form, that we wished to have the honour of paying our court to the Margrave, an officer waited on the D—— of H—— and conducted us to the palace.

There were at dinner the reigning Prince and Princess;—three of their sons, the eldest of whom is married to a Princess of Hesse Darmstadt.—She with one of her sisters was present, also the Princess Dowager of Bareith, daughter to the Duke of Brunswick; two general officers in the imperial service, and other ladies and gentlemen, making in all a company of above thirty at table.

The entertainment was splendid.—The Margrave behaved with the politest attention to the D—— of H——, and with affability to every body.

The Princess of Bareith is of a gay, lively, agreeable character. After dinner the Duke took a view of the different apartments of the palace, and afterwards walked with the Margrave in the gardens till the evening.

The same company were at supper; a band of music played during the repast, and the day went off in a more easy, agreeable manner than I could have expected, considering the number of Princes and Princesses.

The Margrave of Baden Durlach is between forty and fifty years of age. He is a man of learning, good sense, and benevolent disposition. I had heard much, long before I saw him, of his humanity and attention to the well-being of his subjects. This made me view him with a cordial regard, which his rank alone could not have commanded.

He speaks the English language with considerable facility, and is well acquainted with our best authors. Solicitous that his son should enjoy the same advantages, he has engaged Mr. Cramer, a young gentleman from Scotland, of an excellent character, who has been for several years at this court as tutor and companion to the young Prince.

The German Princes are minute observers of form. The same establishment for their household, the same officers in the palace, are to be found here, as in the court of the most powerful monarch in Europe.—The difference lies more in the salaries than in the talents requisite for these places; one Paymaster for the forces has greater emoluments in England, than a Grand Marechal, a Grand Chamberlain, two Secretaries of State, and half a dozen more of the chief officers of a German court, all taken together.

The Margrave of Baden has body guards who do duty in the palace, foot guards who parade before it; also horse guards and hussars, all of whom are perfectly well equipped and exactly disciplined;—a piece of magnificence which seems to be adopted by this prince, merely in conformity with the custom long established in his country.

He keeps on foot no other troops besides the few which are necessary for this duty at the palace, though his revenue is more considerable, and his finances are in much better order than some Princes in Germany who have little standing armies in constant pay. He has too just an understanding not to perceive that the greatest army he could possibly maintain, could be no defence to his dominions, situated as they are between the powerful states of France and Austria: And probably his principles and disposition prevent him from thinking of filling his coffers by hiring his subjects to foreign powers.

If he were so inclined, there is no manner of doubt that he might sell the persons of his subjects as soldiers, or employ them in any other way he should think proper; for he, as well as the other sovereign Princes in Germany, has an unlimited power over his people. If you ask the question, in direct terms, of a German, he will answer in the negative; and will talk of certain rights which the subjects enjoy; and that they can appeal to the great council or general diet of the empire for relief. But after all his ingenuity and distinctions, you find that the barriers which protect the peasant from the power of the prince, are so very weak, that they are hardly worth keeping up, and that the only security the peasant has for his person or property, must proceed from the moderation, good sense, and justice of his sovereign.

Happy would it be for mankind if this unlimited power were always placed in as equitable hands as those of the Margrave of Baden, who employs it entirely for the good of his subjects, by whom he is adored!

This Prince endeavours, by every means he can devise, to introduce industry and manufactures among his people.—There is a considerable number of English tradesmen here, who make Birmingham work, and instruct the inhabitants in that business. He has also engaged many watch-makers from Geneva to settle here, by granting them encouragements and privileges of every kind, and allows no opportunity to slip unimproved, by which he can promote the comfort and happiness of his people: A prince of such a character is certainly a public blessing, and the people are fortunate who are born under his government; But far more fortunate they who are born under a government which can protect them, independent of the virtues, and in spite of the vices, of their sovereign.

When we left Karlsruch, the Margrave gave orders that we might be allowed to pass by a road lately finished, through a noble forest, several leagues in length. After having traversed this, we fell in with the common posting road, entered the bishop of Spires's territories, passed by the town of that name, proceeded to the Electorate of Palatine, and arrived the same night at Manheim.

All the countries I have mentioned form one rich fertile plain; there are few or no gentlemen's houses to vary the scene; nothing but the palace of the prince and the cottages of the peasants, the gentry living in dependence at court, and the merchants and manufacturers in the towns.

LETTER XLII.

Manheim.

This is generally reckoned one of the most beautiful cities in Germany. The streets are all as straight as arrows, being what they call tirées au cordeau, and intersect each other at right angles. This never fails to please at first, but becomes sooner tiresome than a town built with less regularity. When a man has walked through the town for half a forenoon, his eyes search in vain for variety: the same objects seem to move along with him, as if he had been all the while a ship-board.

They calculate the number of inhabitants at 24,000, including the garrison, which consists of 5000 men. This town has three noble gates, adorned with basso relievos very beautifully executed. The Duke and I walked round the ramparts with ease in the space of an hour. The fortifications are well contrived and in good order, and the town acquires great additional strength from being almost entirely surrounded by the Neckar and the Rhine, and situated in a flat, not commanded by any rising ground. Yet perhaps it would be better that this city were quite open, and without any fortification. An attempt to defend it might prove the destruction of the citizens' houses, and the electoral palace. A palace is injudiciously situated when built within a fortified town, because a threat from the enemy to bombard it, might induce the garrison to surrender.

The Electoral palace is a most magnificent structure, situated at the junction of the Rhine and the Neckar.—The cabinet of natural curiosities, and the collection of pictures, are much vaunted. To examine them was amusing enough:—To describe them would, I fear, be a little tedious.

The Elector himself is a man of taste and magnificence, circumstances in his character, which probably afford more pleasure to himself, and the strangers who pass this way, than to his own subjects.

I accompanied the D—— to one of the officers of the court, whose business it is to present strangers. This gentleman is remarkable for his amazing knowledge in all the mysteries of etiquette. He entertained his Grace with much erudition on this subject.—I never observed the D—— yawn so very much.—When our visit was over, he asserted that it had lasted two hours.— Upon examining his watch, he discovered that he had made a mistake of one hour and forty minutes only.

We were presented the following day to the Elector and the Electress. He was dressed in the uniform of his guards, seems to be on the borders of fifty, and has a sensible manly countenance, which I am told is the true index of his character.

The Hereditary Prince is a young man of knowledge and good sense. He surprised me by talking of the party-disputes and adventures which have happened of late years in England, of which I found him minutely informed.—Many people in Germany have the English news-papers and political pamphlets regularly transmitted to them. The acrimony and freedom with which the highest characters are treated, astonish and amuse them, and from these they often form very false and extraordinary conclusions with regard to the state of the nation.

As the Elector intends soon to visit Italy, great numbers of officers have come hither to pay their duty to their sovereign before he depart for that country. He is much esteemed by his officers, with whom he lives in a very affable manner. There are generally thirty covers every day at his table for them, and the strangers who happen to be at the court of Manheim.

One day at dinner, a kind of buffoon came into the room. He walked round the table, and conversed in a familiar manner with every body present, the princes not excepted. His observations were followed by loud bursts of applause from all whom he addressed. As he spoke in German, I could not judge of his wit, but stared around with the anxiety of countenance natural to a man who sees a whole company ready to die with laughter at a jest which he cannot comprehend. An old officer, who sat near me, was touched with compassion for my situation, and explained in French some of the most brilliant repartees for my private use.

As this good-natured officer did not seem to have a great command of the French language, the whole spirit of the jest was allowed to evaporate during the translation:—At least I could not smell a particle when the process was over. However, as these translations evidently cost him a good deal of trouble, I thought myself obliged to seem delighted with his performance; so I joined in the mirth of the company, and endeavoured to laugh as much as any person at the table.

My interpreter afterwards informed me that this genius was from the Tyrol, that he spoke the German with so peculiar an accent, that whatever he said never failed to set the whole table in a roar; c'est pourquoi, added he, il est en possession d'entrer toujours avec le dessert.

This is the only example that I know remaining of a court fool or licensed jester; an office formerly in all the courts of Europe.

LETTER XLIII.

Manheim.

We made a short jaunt to Heidelberg a few days since. That town is about four leagues from Manheim.

Heidelberg is situated in a hollow on the banks of the Neckar, and is surrounded by charming hills perfectly cultivated.

More cheerful scenes of exuberant fertility are to be seen no where than along the fine chain of hills which begin near this town. The summits of these hills are crowned with trees, and their sides and bottoms are clothed with vines.

The Elector's castle is placed on an eminence, which commands the town, and a view of the valley below; but the castle itself unfortunately is commanded by another eminence too near it, from which this noble building was cannonaded when the whole Palatinate was pillaged and burnt, in consequence of that cruel order of Lewis XIV. too literally executed by Turenne.

The particulars of that dismal scene have been transmitted from father to son, and are still spoke of with horror by the peasantry of this country, among whom the French nation is held in detestation to this day.

While we were in the castle we did not omit visiting the renowned Heidelberg tun; but as it was perfectly empty, it made but a dull and uninteresting appearance.

The inhabitants of the Palatinate are partly Protestants, and partly Roman Catholics, who live here in harmony with each other. The great church at Heidelberg is divided into two apartments, in one of which the Protestants, and in the other, the Papists, perform public worship:—A singular proof of the moderation and coolness of people's minds with regard to a subject that inflamed them so violently in the days of their ancestors.

We remained only one day at Heidelberg, and returned in the evening to this place. The lives and manners of the inhabitants of this city seem to be as uniform and formal as the streets and buildings. No noise, mobs or bustle; at mid-day every thing is as calm and quiet as the streets of London at midnight. This gives one the notion that the citizens are under the same restraint and discipline with the troops.

I have seen these last perform their exercise every morning on the parade. I was a good deal surprised to observe, that not only the movements of the soldiers muskets, and the attitudes of their bodies, but also their devotions, were under the direction of the major's cane. The following motions are performed as part of the military manœuvres every day before the troops are marched to their different guards.

The major flourishes his cane;—the drum gives a single tap, and every man under arms raises his hand to his hat;—at a second stroke on the drum, they take off their hats, and are supposed to pray;—at a third, they finish their petitions, and put their hats on their heads.—If any man has the assurance to prolong his prayer a minute longer than the drum indicates, he is punished on the spot, and taught to be less devout for the future.

The ingenious inventor of drums certainly never dreamt of their becoming the regulators of people's piety.—But the modern improvements in the military art are truly wonderful!—and we need not despair, after this, of seeing a whole regiment, by the progress of discipline, so modelled as to eat, drink, and perform other animal functions, uniformly together, at the word of command, as they poise their firelocks.

LETTER XLIV.

Manheim.

Having left orders at Geneva to forward all our letters of a certain date to Manheim, and to direct those which should come afterwards, to Frankfort on the Maine, I had the good fortune to receive yours last night.

I feel as much indignation as you possibly can, against those who endeavour to hurt the peace of families by malignant publications, and I enter fully into Lord ———'s on so unmerited an attack. Yet I should be heartily sorry to see these evils remedied by any restriction on the freedom of the press; because I am every day more and more convinced that its unrestrained productions, the licentious news-papers themselves not excepted, have conveyed to every corner of Great Britain, along with much impertinence and scurrility, such a regard for the constitution, such a sense of the rights of the subject, and such a degree of general knowledge, as never were so universally diffused over any other nation. Such a law as your friend proposes might, no doubt, protect individuals from unjust attacks in print: but it would at the same time remove one great means of clearing their innocence, and making known their wrongs, when injured in a more essential manner. It would limit the right which every Briton has of publicly addressing his countrymen, when he finds himself injured or oppressed by the perversion of law, or the insolence of office.

Examples might be given of men of great integrity being attacked in the most cruel and ungenerous manner by people high in office and guarded by power. Such men had no other means of redress than that of appealing to the candour and good sense of the public, which they used with success. Every man's observation may suggest to him many kinds of injustice and oppression which the rich, the insidious, or the powerful, can commit in spite of law, or perhaps by the aid of law, against the poor, the unsuspecting, and the friendless.—Many, who can silence conscience and evade law, tremble at the thoughts of their injustice being published; and nothing is, nothing can be, a greater check to the wantonness of power, than the privilege of unfolding private grievances at the bar of the public. For thus the cause of individuals is made a public concern, and the general indignation which their wrongs excite, forms at once one of the severest punishments which can be inflicted on the oppressor, and one of the strongest bulwarks that can be raised in defence of the unprotected.

By this means also the most speedy and effectual alarm is given all over the nation when any great public misconduct happens, or upon any appearance of a design against the constitution; and many evils are detected and prevented, which otherwise might have been unobserved, till they had become too strong for remedy. And though this liberty produces much silly advice, and malignant censors without number, it likewise opens the door to some of a different character, who give useful hints to ministers, which would have been lost without the freedom of anonymous publication.

The temporary and partial disorders, which are the consequences of public freedom, have been greatly exaggerated by some people, and represented as more than equivalent to all the advantages resulting from a free government. But if such persons had opportunities of observing the nature of those evils which spring up in absolute governments, they would soon be convinced of their error.

The greatest evil that can arise from the licentiousness which accompanies civil liberty is, that people may rashly take a dislike to liberty herself, from the teasing impertinence and absurdity of some of her real or affected well-wishers; as a man might become less fond of the company of his best friend, if he found him always attended by a snappish cur, which without provocation was always growling and barking.

But to prove the weakness of such conduct, we have only to call to mind that the stream of licentiousness perhaps never rose higher than it did some years since in England.—And what were the mighty evils that followed?—Many respectable characters were grossly misrepresented in printed publications.—Certain daring scribblers evaded the punishment they deserved:—Many windows were broken, and the chariots of a few members of parliament were bespattered with dirt by the mob.—What are these frivolous disorders when compared to the gloomy regularity produced by despotism; in which men are obliged to the most painful circumspection in all their actions; are afraid to speak their sentiments on the most common occurrences; suspicious of cherishing government spies in their household servants; distrustful of their own relations and most intimate companions, and at all times exposed to the oppression of men in power, and to the insolence of their favourites?—No confusion, in my mind, can be more terrible than the stern disciplined regularity and vaunted police of arbitrary governments, where every heart is depressed by fear, where mankind dare not assume their natural characters, where the free spirit must crouch to the slave in office, where genius must repress her effusions, or, like the Egyptian worshippers, offer them in sacrifice to the calves of power; and where the human mind, always in shackles, shrinks from every generous effort.

LETTER XLV.

Mentz.

We left Manheim five or six days ago. It is very easy travelling through this part of Germany, the roads being perfectly good, and the country a continued plain. From Basil to within a few miles of Mentz, the posting road does not make even the most gentle ascent; a vast length of country to be all along a perfect level.

By the great numbers of Monks and Friars, of all colours and conditions, that are to be met near this city, we were apprised of our entrance into an ecclesiastical state, while the plump persons and rosy complexions of these Fathers sufficiently proved, that they did not live in the fertile land of Rhenish for nothing.

However good Christians they might be, many of them had much the appearance of paying occasional homage to the ancient heathen deity Bacchus, without being restrained in their worship like the soldiers on the parade at Manheim.—One of them in particular appeared to have just arisen from his devotion.—He moved along in the most unconcerned manner imaginable, without observing any direct course, or regarding whether he went to the right hand or to the left. He muttered to himself as he went.— Does he repeat his pater-noster? said I.—I rather imagine he prays from Horace, replied the D——

———Quo me, Bacche, rapis tui

Plenum? Quæ nemora, aut quos agor in specus

Velox mente nova?———

On both sides of the Rhine the ground here begins to become hilly and irregular, forming banks finely exposed to the sun. Here the best Rhenish wine is produced, and even a very small portion of these exuberant banks is of considerable value. A chain of well-inhabited villages runs along from Mentz, by Bacharach, all the way to Coblentz, where the Rhine is joined by the Moselle.

Bacharach is said to derive its name from an altar of Bacchus (Bacchi Ara) supposed to have been erected by the Romans in gratitude for the quantity and quality of the wine produced in the neighbourhood. A little before we entered Mentz, we passed by the Favorita, a beautiful palace belonging to the Elector, situated where the Rhine is joined by the Maine.

Mentz is finely situated, built in an irregular manner, and most plentifully provided with churches. The cathedral is but a gloomy fabric. In this there is what they call a treasury, which contains a number of clumsy jewels, some relics, and a mighty rich wardrobe of priests vestments.

There are some troops in this capital, but I do not think the officers have that smart presumptuous air which generally accompanies men of their profession. They seem conscious that the clergy are their masters; and, I have a notion, are a little out of countenance on that account.

The streets swarm with ecclesiastics, some of them in fine coaches, and attended by a great number of servants. I remarked also many genteel airy abbés; who, one could easily see, were the most fashionable people, and give the ton at this place.

Though it is most evident that in this electorate the clergy have taken exceeding good care of themselves; yet, in justice to them, it must be acknowledged, that the people also seem to be in an easy situation. The peasantry appear to be in a state of far greater abundance than those of France, or even those in the Elector of Manheim's dominions.

I have some desire to see an ecclesiastical court, and would willingly visit this of Mentz; but the D—— of H——, who seems to have no excessive fondness for any court, says, a court of clergymen must be more dismal and tedious than any other, and I fear will not be prevailed on to appear at this; in which case we shall leave this place to-morrow morning early, without further ceremony.

LETTER XLVI.

Frankfort on the Maine.

We have been here two weeks.—To form a proper judgment of the genius and manners of any nation, it is necessary to live familiarly with the inhabitants for a considerable time; but a smaller degree of observation will suffice to give a pretty just idea of the nature of its government. The chilling effects of despotic oppression, or the benign influence of freedom and commerce, strike the eye of the most careless traveller.

The streets of Frankfort are spacious and well-paved; the houses stately, clean, and convenient; the shops well furnished; the dress, the numbers, the air, and general manners of the inhabitants, sufficiently show, without other information, that there is no little despot within their walls, to impoverish them in support of his grandeur, and to put every action of their lives, every movement of their bodies, under restraint by his caprice.

The houses are of brick, but have a better appearance than brick houses in general, owing chiefly to their being covered with a kind of reddish stucco, which is come into use here of late, and, it is believed, will render the buildings more durable. The fronts of many of the finest are also adorned with bas reliefs, of white stucco, in imitation of marble. These white ornaments, on the red ground, form too strong a contrast, and do not please an eye fond of simplicity. But the Germans, in general, have a taste for showy ornament, in their dress, furniture, and houses. Frankfort is a free imperial city, having a small territory belonging to it, and is governed by its own magistracy.

All religions are tolerated here, under certain restrictions; but Lutheranism is the established faith, as the magistrates are of that communion.

The principal church is in the possession of the Roman Catholics, but no public procession of the host is permitted through the streets. All the ceremonies of their religion are confined to the houses of individuals, or performed within the walls of this church. In it there is a chapel, to which the emperor is conducted immediately after his election, in order to be crowned by the Elector of Mentz.

The Jews have a synagogue in this city, where they perform their religious rites; but the Calvinists have never been allowed any public house of worship within the territory of Frankfort. They attend divine service at a place called Bockenheim in the county of Hanau, where they have built a church.

This is but unkind treatment; and it seems, at first sight, a little extraordinary, that Martin Luther should show more indulgence to his old enemy Lord

Peter, and even to Judas Iscariot himself, than to his fellow-reformer John Calvin.

Though Frankfort is thought a fine town, and the effect produced by the whole is magnificent, yet there are no buildings in particular worthy of attention. It is expected, however, that all strangers should visit the town-house, and see the chamber where the Emperor is elected. And it would be reckoned a great want of curiosity, not to see the famous golden bull which is kept there with the utmost care. A sight of this costs a golden ducat; a sufficient price for a glance of an old manuscript, which not one person in a hundred can read, and still fewer can understand.

A countryman of ours, who expected more amusement for his money, complained loudly of this as an imposition, and on hearing a German talk of the high price which every thing bore in England, he retorted on him in these words:—Il n'y a rien en Angleterre si cher que votre *taureau* d'or à Frankfort.

There is a custom observed here, which I shall mention on account of its singularity, though I enquired in vain for its origin. Two women appear every day at noon on the battlements of the principal steeple, and play some very solemn airs with trumpets. This music is accompanied by vocal psalmody, performed by four or five men, who always attend the female trumpeters for that purpose.

The people here have a violent taste for psalm-singing. There are a considerable number of men and boys, who have this for their only profession. They are engaged by some families to officiate two or three times a week in the morning, before the master and mistress of the family get out of bed.

When any person in tolerable circumstances dies, a band of these sweet singers assemble in the streets before the house, and chant an hour every day to the corpse, till it is interred. The same band accompanies the funeral, singing hymns all the way.

Funerals are conducted with an uncommon degree of solemnity in this town:—A man clothed in a black cloak, and carrying a crucifix, at the end of a long pole, leads the procession:—A great number of hired mourners in the same dress, and each with a lemon in his hand, march after him:—Then come the singers, followed by the corpse in a hearse; and lastly, the relations in mourning coaches.

The crucifix is carried in this manner at all funerals, whether the deceased has died a Roman Catholic, a Lutheran, or a Calvinist. That this custom should be followed by the two latter, surprised me a good deal. I should have imagined that the Calvinists in particular, whatever they did with the lemons, would never have been able to digest the crucifix.

There is a very considerable number of Calvinists in this place; it is generally thought they are the most industrious. They unquestionably are the richest part of the inhabitants. This may be partly owing to a circumstance that some of them consider as a hardship—their being excluded from any share in the government of the city.—Many of the Calvinist families are descendents of French Protestants, who left their country at the revocation of the edict of Nantz.

There are some villages near Frankfort consisting entirely of French refugees; who, deserting their country at the same time, have settled here in a cluster. Their descendents speak French in their common conversation, and retain many of their original customs to this hour.

Two or three families now living at Frankfort are of English origin. Their predecessors fled first to Holland, during the persecutions in the reign of Mary, and being afterwards driven out of that country by the cruelty of the Duke of Alva, they at length found an asylum for themselves, and their posterity, in this free imperial city.

The number of Jews in Frankfort is prodigious, considering one dismal inconvenience they are subjected to, being obliged to live all together in a single street built up at one end:—There is a large gate at the other, which is regularly shut at a certain hour of the night, after which no Jews dare appear in the streets; but the whole herd must remain cooped and crowded together, like so many black cattle, till morning. As this street is narrow, the room allotted for each family small, and as the children of Israel were never remarkable for their cleanliness, and always noted for breeding, the Jews quarter, you will believe, is not the sweetest part of the town. I scarce think they could have been worse lodged in the land of Egypt.

They have several times made offer of considerable sums to the magistrates of Frankfort for liberty to build or purchase another street for their accommodation; but all such proposals have hitherto been rejected.

The Jews in Frankfort are obliged to fetch water when a fire happens in any part of the city, and the magistrates in return permit them to choose judges out of their own body for deciding disputes among themselves; but if either party refuses to submit to this, an appeal is open to the magistrates.

They must unquestionably enjoy some great advantages by the trade they carry on, to compensate for such inconveniencies. During the day-time they are allowed the liberty of walking all over the town; a privilege which they improve with equal assiduity and address. They attack you in the street, ply at the gate of your lodgings, and even glide into your apartments, offering to supply you with every commodity you can have occasion for: And if you happen to pass by the entrance of their street, they intreat your custom with the violence and vociferation of so many Thames watermen.

I was twice at their synagogue. There is nothing magnificent in their worship; but much apparent zeal and fervour. I saw one of their most important rites performed on two children. It was impossible not to feel compassion for the poor infants, thus cruelly initiated into a community, who had formerly the misfortune of being despised by the Heathens, and now are execrated by all pious Christians.

LETTER XLVII.

Frankfort on the Maine.

You will be surprised at our remaining so long at a place where there is no court, and few of those entertainments which allure and retain travellers. The truth is, the D—— of H—— seems fond of this place; and as for my own part, I have formed an acquaintance with some very worthy people here, whose friendship I shall take every occasion to cultivate.

Society here is divided into Noblesse and the Bourgeois. The first consists of some noble families from various parts of Germany, who have chosen Frankfort for their residence, and a few original citizens of Frankfort, but who have now obtained the rank of nobility. The citizens who connect themselves with strangers, have made their fortunes by commerce, which some of them still follow.

There is a public assembly for the nobility once a week, at which they drink tea, converse, or play at cards from six to ten. On the other nights, the same company meet alternately at each other's houses, and pass the evening in the same manner. None of the Bourgeois families are invited to these parties; but they have assemblies of the same kind among themselves, and often entertain their friends, and the strangers with whom they are acquainted, in a very hospitable manner at their tables. The noblemen who reside in Frankfort, and the nobility of all degrees, and of every nation, who accidentally pass through it, cheerfully accept of these invitations to dine with the citizens, but none of the German ladies of quality condescend so far. While their fathers, husbands, and brothers, are entertained at a Bourgeois table, they chuse rather to dine at home by themselves; and they certainly judge wisely, if they prefer a spare diet to good cheer.

The distinction of ranks is observed in Germany, with all the scrupulous precision that a matter of that importance deserves. There is a public concert in this place supported by subscription. One would imagine that the subscribers would take their seats as they entered the room, that those who came earliest would have their choice.—No such matter.—The two first rows are kept for the ladies of quality, and the wives and daughters of the citizens must be contented to sit behind, let them come at what hour, and pay what money they please.—After all, this is not so bad as in an assembly of nobility, where commons are not permitted to sit, even in the lobby, whatever price they may have paid for their seat in parliament.

Since we arrived, the theatre has been opened for the winter, by a troop of German comedians. I was there the first night; previous to the play, there was a kind of allegorical prologue, intended as a compliment to the magistrates of Frankfort. This was performed by Justice, Wisdom, and Plenty, each of whom appeared in person, with the usual attributes. The last was very properly personated by a large fat woman, big with child. As to the two former, I hope, for the sake of the good people of Frankfort, that they are better represented in the town-council, than they were on the stage. This prologue was concluded by a long harangue pronounced by the plumpest Apollo, I dare venture to say, that ever appeared in the heavens above, or on the earth beneath.

After this the play began, which was a German translation of the English play of George Barnwell, with considerable alterations. Barnwell is represented as an imprudent young man; but he does not murder his uncle, as in the English play, or commit any gross crime; the German translator therefore, instead of hanging, only marries him at the end of the piece.

Most of the plays represented on the German stage, are translations from the English or French; for Germany, so fertile in writers in divinity, jurisprudence, medicine, chymistry, and other parts of natural philosophy, has produced few poets till of late.

> Jam nova progenies cœlo demittitur alto,

and the German muse is now admired all over Europe. Her beauties are felt and applauded by men of genius, even through the medium of a translation, which is a strong proof of her original energy. It must, however, be a great discouragement to German poetry in general, and to the dramatic in particular, that the French language prevails in all the courts, and that French plays are represented there in preference to German.

The native language of the country is treated like a vulgar and provincial dialect, while the French is cultivated as the only proper language for people of fashion.—Children of the first families are instructed in French, before they acquire their mother-tongue, and pains are taken to keep them ignorant of this, that it may not hurt their pronunciation of the other. I have met with people who considered it as an accomplishment to be unable to express themselves in the language of their country, and who have pretended to be more ignorant, in this particular, than they were in reality.

I have been assured by many, who understand the German language well, that it is nervous, copious, most expressive, and capable of all the graces of poetry. The truth of this appears by the works of several late writers, who have endeavoured to check this unnatural prejudice in their countrymen, and to restore the language of their ancestors to its native honours.—But what are the efforts of good sense, taste, and genius, in opposition to fashion, and the influence of courts?

Among the winter amusements of this place, traineau parties may be reckoned. These can take place in the time of frost only, and when there is a considerable quantity of snow upon the ground. I had an opportunity of seeing a very splendid entertainment of this kind lately, which was given by some young gentlemen to an equal number of ladies.

A traineau is a machine in the shape of a horse, lion, swan; or in that of a griffin, unicorn, or some other fanciful form, without wheels; but made below like a sledge, for the conveniency of sliding over the snow. Some are gilded, and otherwise ornamented, according to the whim of the proprietor.—A pole stands up from one side, to which an ensign or flag is fastened, which waves over the heads of those placed on the machine. The lady, wrapped in fur, sits before, and the gentleman stands behind on a board made for that purpose.

The whole is drawn by two horses, which are either conducted by a postillion, or driven by the gentleman.—The horses are gaudily ornamented, and have bells hanging from the trappings which cover them.

This party consisted of about thirty traineaus, each attended by two or three servants on horseback with flambeaux; for this amusement was taken when it began to grow dark.—One traineau took the lead;—the rest followed at a convenient distance in a line, and drove for two or three hours through the principal streets and squares of Frankfort.—The horses go at a brisk trot or canter; the motion of the traineau is easy and agreeable; the bells, ensigns, and torches, make a very gay and showy appearance, which seemed to be much relished by the parties immediately concerned, and admired by the spectators.

A few days after this exhibition, as we were preparing to set out for Hanau in a traineau, Mr. S———, brother to Lord S———, arrived at the inn. Though he had travelled for two days and nights, without having been in bed, he was so little fatigued, that he went along with us. Hanau is some leagues distant from Frankfort. We had a full proof of the smooth movement of the traineau, which, in the time of frost, and when there is a proper quantity of snow on the ground, is certainly the most delightful way of travelling that can possibly be imagined.

Hanau is the residence of the Hereditary Prince of Hesse Cassel. As we entered the town we met the Princess, who is sister-in-law to the King of Denmark. She, with some of the ladies of the court, was taking the air also in a traineau.

Besides the troops of Hanau, two regiments of Hanoverians are there at present. The Hereditary Prince is not on the best terms with his father. He lives here, however, in a state of independency, possessed of the revenues of this country, which is guaranteed to him by the Kings of Britain, Denmark, and Prussia: but there is no intercourse between this little court and that of Hesse Cassel.

After dinner we returned to Frankfort. The D—— prevailed with Mr. S—— to remain a longer time at Frankfort than he had intended. He is a sensible young man of spirit and ambition. His grandfather, the old Earl of D——, endeavours to seduce him into holy orders, promising him a living of 2000l. a year, which is in the gift of the family. This you will acknowledge to be a temptation which few younger brothers could withstand. Nature, however, seems to have destined this young gentleman for another line in life. My own opinion is, he would rather have the command of a troop of dragoons, than be promoted to the See of Canterbury.

LETTER XLVIII.

Frankfort.

Some of the nobility who reside in this city, take every opportunity of pointing out the essential difference that there is, and the distinctions that ought to be made, between their families and those of the Bourgeois, who, though they have, by commerce or some profession equally ignoble, attained great wealth, which enables them to live in a stile of magnificence unbecoming their rank; yet their noble neighbours insinuate, that they always retain a vulgarity of sentiment and manners, unknown to those whose blood has flowed pure through several generations, unmixed with that puddle which stagnates in the veins of plebeians.

The D—— of H—— does not seem to have studied natural philosophy with accuracy sufficient to enable him to observe this distinction. He mingles in the societies of the citizens, with as much ease and alacrity, as in those of the nobility, dining with the one, and drinking coffee with the other, in the most impartial manner, and between the two he contrives to amuse himself tolerably well.

The two families with which we are in the greatest degree of intimacy, are those of Mons. de Barkhause, and Mons. P. Gogle. The former is a principal person in the magistracy, a man of learning and worth. His lady is of a noble family in the dukedom of Brunswic, a woman of admirable good sense and many accomplishments. She is well acquainted with English and French literature. The French language she speaks like a native, and though she cannot converse in English without difficulty, she understands and relishes the works of some of our best authors.

Mr. Gogle has travelled over the greatest part of Europe, and is equally acquainted with men and books. He has made a plentiful fortune by commerce, and lives in a very agreeable and hospitable manner.

In these two houses we occasionally meet with the best company of both the classes of society in this place, and in one or other when there is no public assembly we generally pass the afternoon.—The former part of the day (a thaw having lately dissolved the snow) we often pass in jaunts to the environs of this place, which are very beautiful.

As the D—— of H—— and I were riding one day along the banks of the Maine, near the village of Heix, which is in the territories of the Elector of Mentz, we observed a building which seemed to be the residence of some prince, or bishop at least. We were surprised we never had heard it spoken of, as it had a more magnificent appearance than any modern building we had seen since our arrival in Germany. We rode up, and upon entering it, found that the apartments within, though not laid out in the best taste, seemed to correspond, in point of expence, with the external appearance.

We were informed by the workmen, who were employed in finishing these apartments, that this palace belonged to a tobacconist in Frankfort, where he still kept shop, and had accumulated a prodigious fortune by making and selling snuff.

Near to the principal house, there is another great building intended for a workhouse, in which tobacco is to be manufactured, with many apartments for the workmen, and vaulted cellars in which the various kinds of snuff are to be kept moist, till sent for inland sale to Frankfort, or shipped on the Maine for foreign markets.

The owner informed us, there were exactly three hundred rooms in both buildings, and the greater number of these belonged to the dwelling-house. We did not chuse to puzzle the man by difficult questions, and therefore refrained from enquiring, what use he intended to make of such an amazing number of rooms, which seemed rather contrived as barracks for two or three thousand soldiers, than any other purpose.

On our return to town, we were informed that this person, who is not a native of Frankfort, though he has been many years established there, had applied to the magistrates for liberty to purchase a certain spot of ground, on which he proposed to build a dwelling-house, &c. which cannot be done by any but citizens, without the consent of the council. This being refused, he bought a little piece of land in the territory of Mentz, immediately beyond that of Frankfort, and on the banks of the Maine; and being highly piqued by the refusal he had met with from the magistrates, he had reared a building greatly larger and more extensive than was necessary, or than he at first had intended, in the full persuasion that the remorse of the magistrates would be in proportion to the size of this fabric.

The tobacconist has already expended fifty thousand pounds on this temple of vengeance, and his wrath against the magistrates seems to be yet unappeased—for he still lavishes his money with a rancour against these unfortunate men, that is very unbecoming a Christian. The inhabitants of Frankfort, while they acknowledge the imprudence of the magistrates, do not applaud the wisdom of their antagonist, in whose brain they assert there must be some apartments as empty as any in the vast structure he is building.

Another day his Grace and I rode to Bergen, a small village which has been rendered eminent by the attempt made there by Prince Ferdinand on the French army in the year 1759.

We were accompanied by the Messrs. de Lessener, two gentlemen, now retired from the service, and living at Frankfort, who had been in the action, one a Captain in the Hanoverian army, the other of the same rank in the French.

During the winter of that memorable year, you may remember that the French, with more policy than justice, had seized upon this neutral city, and established their head-quarters here. This was attended by great advantages, securing to them the course of the Maine and Upper Rhine, by which they received supplies from Strasbourg, and all the intermediate cities.

Prince Ferdinand having formed the design of driving them from this advantageous situation, before they could be reinforced, suddenly assembled his army, which was cantoned about Munster, and after three days of forced marches, came in sight of the French army, at that time commanded by the Duke de Broglio, who, having received intelligence of the Prince's scheme, had made a very judicious disposition.

On the forenoon of the 13th of April, the Prince began his attack on the right wing of the French army, which occupied the village of Bergen.—This was renewed with great vivacity three several times. The Prince of Isembourg, and about 1500 of the Allies, fell in the action, which was prolonged till the evening; Prince Ferdinand then determining to draw off his troops, made such a disposition as persuaded the enemy he intended a general attack next morning—and by this means he accomplished his retreat in the night, without being harassed by the French.

I have heard officers of great merit assert, that nothing could be more judiciously planned and executed, than this enterprise; the only one of importance, however, in which that great General failed during the whole war.

By this misfortune the allied army were reduced to great difficulties, and the progress of the French, with the continued retreat of the Allies, spread such an alarm over the Electorate of Hanover, that many individuals sent their most valuable effects to Stade, from whence they might be conveyed to England.—The affairs of the Allies were soon after re-established by the decisive victory of Minden, which raised the military character of Prince Ferdinand higher than ever; though officers of penetration, who were at both actions, are still of opinion, that his talents were to the full as conspicuous at Bergen, where he was repulsed, as at the glorious field of Minden, by which Hanover and Brunswick were preserved, and the French obliged to abandon almost all Westphalia.

LETTER XLIX.

Frankfort.

I returned a few days since from Darmstadt, having accompanied the D—— of H—— on a visit which he made to that court.

The reigning Prince of Hesse Darmstadt not being there, we were directed to pay our first visit to the Princess Maximilian, his aunt.—She invited us the same evening to play at cards and sup with her.—There were about ten people at table.—The Princess was gay, affable, and talkative.—The D—— confessed he never had passed an evening so agreeably with an old woman in his life.

Next morning we went to the parade, which is an object of great attention at this place. The Prince has a most enthusiastic passion for military manœuvres and evolutions.—Drilling and exercising his soldiers are his chief amusements, and almost his sole employment. That he may enjoy this in all kinds of weather, and at every season of the year, he has built a room sufficiently capacious to admit 1500 men, to perform their exercise in it all together.

This room is accommodated with sixteen stoves, by which it may be kept at the exact degrees of temperature which suits his Highness's constitution.—On the morning that we were present, there was only the ordinary guard, consisting of three hundred men, who having performed their exercises, and marched for an hour up and down this spacious Gymnasium, were divided into parties and detached to their respective posts.

The Darmstadt soldiers are tall, tolerably clothed, and above all things remarkably well powdered. They go through their manœuvres with that dexterity which may be expected of men who are continually employed in the same action, under the eye of their prince, who is an admirable judge, and severe critic in this part of the military art.

There is no regular fortification round this town; but a very high stone-wall, which is not intended to prevent an enemy from entering, being by no means adequate to such a purpose; but merely designed to hinder the garrison from deserting, to which they are exceedingly inclined; these poor men taking no delight in the warlike amusements which constitute the supreme joy of their sovereign.

Centinels are placed at small distances all round the wall, who are obliged to be exceedingly alert. One soldier gives the words *all is well* in German, to his neighbour on the right, who immediately calls the same to the centinel beyond him, and so it goes round till the first soldier receives the words from the left, which he transmits to the right as formerly, and so the call circulates without any intermission through the whole night.

Every other part of garrison duty is performed with equal exactness, and all neglects as severely punished as if an enemy were at the gates.

The men are seldom more than two nights out of three in bed. This, with the attention requisite to keep their clothes and accoutrements clean, is very hard duty, especially at present, when the frost is uncommonly keen, and the ground covered with snow.

There is a small body of cavalry at Darmstadt just now. They are dressed in buff coats, and magnificently accoutred.—These are the horse-guards of the prince.—Few as they are, I never saw so many men together of such a height in my life, none of them being under six English feet three inches high, and several of them considerably above that enormous stature.

The Prince of Hesse Darmstadt formerly kept a greater number of troops: At present his whole army does not exceed five thousand men. But as the conduct of princes, however judicious it may be, seldom passes uncensured, there are people who blame him for entertaining even this number. They declare, that this prince's finances, being in very great disorder, cannot support this establishment; which, though small, may be counted high, considering the extent of his dominions. They insist also upon the loss, which agriculture and manufactures must sustain, by having the stoutest men taken away from these necessary employments, and their strength exhausted in useless parade. For these rigid censors have the assurance to assert, that an army of five thousand men, though burdensome to the country, is not sufficient to defend it; that the number is by far too great for amusement, and infinitely too small for any manner of use.

The same day, we dined with the Princess Maximilian, and in the afternoon were presented to Prince George's family. He is brother to the reigning Prince. He happened to be indisposed; but his princess received the D—— with the utmost politeness.

Their two youngest sons and three daughters were at supper. The former are still very young; the latter are well-looking, remarkably accomplished, and do much credit to the great pains their mother has bestowed on their education.

Next morning we were invited to breakfast, by the Baron Riedesal, at a pleasant country-house he has near Darmstadt.—His G—— went with him, in a carriage of a very particular construction. The Baron sat on a low seat next the horses, and drove; the D—— in a higher place behind him. Each of these is made for one person only; but behind all, there was a wooden seat, in the shape of a little horse, on which two servants were mounted. The usual posting-chaises in this country hold six persons with ease; and people even of the first rank generally have two or three servants in the chaise with them. In point of œconomy, these carriages are well imagined; and, in the time of frost, not inconvenient; for here travellers take special care to fortify themselves against cold by cloaks lined with fur. But when it rains hard, two of the company at least must be drenched; for the German chaises are never intirely covered above.

I went with Count Cullemberg in his coach. We passed the forenoon very agreeably at this house, which seems to be advantageously situated; but in its present snowy dress, one can no more judge of the natural complexion of the country, than of that of an actress new-painted for the stage.

We dined with Prince George, who was sufficiently recovered to be at table. He is a handsome man, of a soldier-like appearance, and has all the ease and openness of the military character.

His second son, who had been absent for some weeks, arrived while we were at table. He is a fine young man, about eighteen years of age. It was pleasing to observe the satisfaction which this small incident diffused over the faces of father, mother, and the whole family, which formed a groupe worthy the pencil of Greuse.

Do not suspect that I am prejudiced in favour of this family, merely because they belong to a prince.—An appearance of domestic happiness is always agreeable, whether we find it in a palace or a cottage; and the same symptoms of good humour, though they would not have surprised me so much, would have delighted me equally in the family of a peasant.

END OF THE FIRST VOLUME.

Milton Keynes UK
Ingram Content Group UK Ltd.
UKHW030852011224
451361UK00001B/68